Benjamin J. Willard

Captain Ben's Book

Benjamin J. Willard

Captain Ben's Book

ISBN/EAN: 9783337081126

Printed in Europe, USA, Canada, Australia, Japan

Cover: Foto ©ninafisch / pixelio.de

More available books at **www.hansebooks.com**

A RECORD OF THE THINGS WHICH HAPPENED TO

Capt. Benjamin J. Willard,

PILOT AND STEVEDORE,

DURING SOME SIXTY YEARS ON SEA AND LAND,

AS RELATED BY HIMSELF.

COPYRIGHT, 1895, BY CAPT. B. J. WILLARD,
PORTLAND, MAINE.

DEDICATION.

TO the ship-masters, merchants, and ship-brokers whose patronage, during forty-one years, has made possible the employment and the experience recorded in these pages, I gratefully dedicate my book.

B. J. WILLARD.

PREFACE.

I HAVE been asked many times to tell my story, and have at last concluded to do so. It is the "plain, unvarnished tale" of a man who has passed his life on and along the stormy Atlantic coast, sometime on sea and sometime on shore, and who has met the perils incident to the experience of a sailor and a pilot. Most people of English blood, whether inland bred or brought up within the sound of the waves, take pleasure in tales of the sea, however homely they may be told; and for them my book is written. That they may find the same enjoyment in reading that I have had in writing it, is the earnest hope of

BENJAMIN J. WILLARD.

TABLE OF CONTENTS.

CHAPTER I.

Cradled in a Boat — Earliest Recollections — Catching the First Shark — A Mammoth Cod — My Trip to the Georges Bank and How I Lost My Black Stockings — The Hampton Boat and the White Head Boiling Springs — Lobster Catching Fifty Years Ago, . 15

CHAPTER II.

The Harbor in a Fog — Old Time Hospitality on the Cape — My First Chew of Tobacco — An Ancient School-House — How Fishermen Came To Use Compasses — The Harm Done to Hook Fishing by Seines and Seals, 23

CHAPTER III.

The Loss of the Pleasure Boat "Leo" in Casco Bay — Death by Downing of a Woman and Eight Children — Living on Cracker Crumbs in the Bay of Fundy — Whimsical Adventure near Biddeford Pool — A Perilous Passage from Philadelphia to Portland. 29

CHAPTER IV.

In Which I Become a Ship-Owner — The Great April Gale of 1851 — Riding It Out in Little Egg Harbor — The Race from Philadelphia to Portland — Forsaking Sea for Land Service. 36

CHAPTER V.

In Which I Become a Stevedore and Subsequently a Pilot — Taking the Allan Steamships into Port — Piloting a Bonded Vessel, and the Trouble It Brought — How I Was Unjustly Put in Jail, and My Experiences There — An Appeal for Long-Delayed Justice — Some Amusing Experiences. . 48

CHAPTER VI.

In Which a Sword-Fish is Harpooned — It Proves a Novelty in Portland — How I Piloted a Disabled Steamer into Port — The Perilous Experience of a Pilot — Pulling Drowning Men out of the Water — A Famous Camping-Out Club — Hen Hawks for Dinner — The Father of the Finnan Haddie Industry and His Skill at Quoits.   57

CHAPTER VII.

Portland Harbor in War Time — Much Tangled Red Tape — Rushing Associated Press News to the Shore — Perilous Experience of a Coast Pilot — The Close Shave of the Anglo Saxon — Sudden Death of my Father,   67

CHAPTER VIII.

Capture of the "Caleb Cushing" and the "Archer" by Confederate Privateers — The Bold Attempt in Portland Harbor — A Day of Excitement in the City — Soldiers and Citizens to the Rescue — Blowing up of the "Cushing" and Recapture of the "Archer" — Confederate Prisoners in Fort Preble — How Daniel Gould Came to His Death,   74

CHAPTER IX.

The Confederate Account of the Capture of the "Caleb Cushing" — Mr. Hunt's Vivacious Story — How the Privateers Stole into the Harbor, Stole Out, and Were Caught with the Goods in Their Possession — The Fish Chowder on Board the "Archer," and the Humble Pie the Privateers Afterwards Ate,   82

CHAPTER X.

The Wreck of the Bohemian — Scenes and Incidents of that Memorable Disaster — How the Ill-Fated Steamer Went Ashore — A Notable Campaign Orator among the Survivors — Fishing Up Cases of Goods — Mr. Farmer, Captain Sargent, and the Cook Stove — The Diver Who Took a Nap at the Bottom of the Sea.   87

CHAPTER XI.

Deep-Sea Fishing—The Nervous Man and His Gun—Capturing a Dusky Shark—The Adventure of the Scotchman and the Whale—My Trained Pets, the Coach Dog and the Cedar Bird. . . 95

CHAPTER XII.

A Whale in the Harbor—The Seven-Ton Blackfish—How a Hayseed Spoiled His Linen Trowsers—Appearance and Habits of the Blackfish—A Lively Fight with a Sword-Fish—The Summer of 1867, . . 110

CHAPTER XIII.

In Which All Manner of Fish is Sought, from Sea Serpent to Mackerel—A Fight Between a Sword-Fish and Two Killers—St. Elmo's Fire—The Race Between the "Nettle" and "Sparkle"—A Famous Trouting Party on Mount Desert—Concerning Water-Spouts—Hunting Eider Ducks—Doctor Bowles and the White-Tailed Martin—The Beginning of the Sword-Fish Industry, . . 118

CHAPTER XIV.

A Cruise for the Sea Serpent—Distinguished Jurists and Clergymen Hunting the Whale—Lots of Fun but No Fish—A Colored Cook Who Turned White—Collecting Ship News for the Daily Papers—Rescue of a Gunning Party on Half Way Rock—Captain Senter and the "Sparkle," . . 129

CHAPTER XV.

The Peabody Obsequies—Arrival of the "Monarch" off Portland and Severe Trip of the Pilot Boat in Search of Her—The Impressive Naval Procession up the Harbor.—Admiral Farragut and the "Terror"—Another Great Naval Pageant—The Duke of Newcastle's Hat, . . 136

CHAPTER XVI.

I Become an Inventor and Patent a Life Preserver—Another Fruitless Search for the Sea Serpent—A Funny Fourth of

July in Portland—How the Hand-Organs played in Lincoln Park—An Earnest Plea for Light-House Improvement, . 141

CHAPTER XVII.

Days When a Hogshead of Coal Lasted Portland a Whole Season Mr. Samuel E. Spring and the Government Sale of Cigars- Gunning on Richmond Island — Formation of the Willard Shooting Association Pat and the Loon, . 150

CHAPTER XVIII.

How the " Brooklyn " Struck on Hog Island Ledge — Old Neptune Visits the Pilot Boat " Maggie " and Shaves the Passengers— Mr. Strout's Encounter with a Sword-Fish- Something About Spanish Mackerel, . 159

CHAPTER XIX.

The Schooner " B. J. Willard " and Her Fortunes—How Steamers Have Taken the Freights from Sailing Vessels — The Way in Which I Celebrated the Portland Centennial — About the Water Boat " Fannie G." — Sunfish and Their Curious Formation, . 169

CHAPTER XX.

The First Tow-Boat in Portland—Changed Conditions of Ocean Traffic—The Blue Shark and His Pursuit — Wild Geese Shooting — A Notable Sword-Fish Party—The First Prize in Nine Years—Last Deep-Sea-Fishing Trip for the Season, 181

CHAPTER XXI.

Transit Between the Cape and Portland- The Famous Ferry Fight — A Stormy Town-Meeting The Dinner That Cost Five Hundred Dollars a Plate—Cape Elizabeth Electrics— The Island Traffic and the Casco Bay Steamboat Company, 190

ADDENDUM, . 201

LIST OF ILLUSTRATIONS.

	PAGE
CAPT. BENJAMIN J. WILLARD — Frontispiece,	2
THE WILLARD HOMESTEAD, 1813,	17
MINOT'S LEDGE LIGHT-HOUSE, ...	37
BRITISH STEAMSHIP "ANTELOPE," CAPT. JOHN SMITH,	50
SWORD-FISH, ...	58
THE "NETTLE" IN A HIGH WIND, . . .	65
CAPTURE AND BLOWING UP OF THE "CALEB CUSHING," .	75
CAPT. JOHN LISCOMB,	77
ONE OF SPOT'S TRICKS,	94
DUSKY MANEATER SHARK,	96
HEAD TRICK, . . .	98
CAPTAIN WILLARD AND HIS DOG SPOT,	100
CAPTAIN WILLARD BATTLING WITH A WHALE, .	102
DOG AND BIRD TRICK, .	104
SPOT SPELLING HIS NAME,	105
DOG AND BIRD TRICK,	107
CHAIR TRICK,	108
BLACKFISH, .	111
ST. ELMO'S FIRE, ,	121
WATER-SPOUTS, .	125
CAPT. WILLIAM SENTER, .	134
LIFE-PRESERVER, . .	142
J. N. MARTIN, PRESIDENT OF THE WILLARD SHOOTING ASSOCIATION,	155
CAPTAIN WILLARD AS NEPTUNE, ...	160
PILOT BOAT "MAGGIE," CAPT. EDWARD L. PARSONS,	162
THE SPANISH MACKEREL, . .	167
THE SCHOONER "B. J. WILLARD,"	170

Steam Water Boat "Fannie G.," Capt. Daniel Peterson, 1883,	175
Sunfish,	178
Tow-Boat "Tiger," the First Tow-Boat in Portland,	182
Capt. B. J. Willard's Cottage, Peaks Island, 1884,	185
Capt. B. J. Willard Trap Shooting, June, 1895,	197
A Shoal of Porpoises,	199
Oak Tree at Horsmonden,	202
Horsmonden Church, Where Simon Willard Was Christened, April 5, 1605,	205

CHAPTER I.

CRADLED IN A BOAT.—EARLIEST RECOLLECTIONS.—CATCHING THE FIRST SHARK.—A MAMMOTH COD.—MY TRIP TO THE GEORGES BANK AND HOW I LOST MY BLACK STOCKINGS.—THE HAMPTON BOAT AND THE WHITE HEAD BOILING SPRINGS.—LOBSTER CATCHING FIFTY YEARS AGO.

I WAS born October 30, 1828, at Simonton's Cove, Cape Elizabeth, Me., cradled in a fishing boat, and brought up to be a fisherman; so that my earliest recollections are all of the sea.

My first fishing trip was made in 1836, when I was not quite eight years old; and though I caught but forty-seven mackerel, while my father caught between two and three barrels, my catch was thought a big one for so small a boy, and I felt very proud of my first success. The next spring my father bought a small fishing schooner with a pink stern, called the "Lively," which he kept two years, at times going to Damariscove Island Harbor, Mackerel Cove in Harpswell, and New Meadows Bay; though Richmond's Island was often visited, it being the best place to set nets over night for bait. White Head Ground and Drunken Ledge were noted for good fishing, particularly cod, when the different schools of fish migrated northward

The "Lively" proving too small, my father, in the spring of 1840, bought the schooner "Martha Washington," a large, able schooner for those days. She also had a pink stern — indeed at that time no others were to be seen. I was then about twelve years old, and felt myself a big boy, though not above a little fun which sometimes led me into scrapes. One day, on the schooner, father and the crew turned in for an afternoon nap, as they expected to be fishing for hake that night, and left me on the lookout. Looking for fun I threw overboard some fish livers and tolled up a large flock of hag-dolls; then baited a mackerel line at which they bit fast. These birds bite hard and fight like an eagle. I tossed them into an empty barrel, where they fought fiercely in their struggles to get out. Such a noise I never heard before or since. The crew were wakened, and soon tumbled on deck, unable to sleep. At my father's orders I tossed the birds overboard. That was my last attempt to catch hag-dolls.

My First Shark.— One night while I was doing boy's duty on the dog watch, from 6 to 8 in the evening, and amusing myself by catching squid, I saw a big fish swimming round which soon stole my bait. The water was sparkling with phosphorus and I could see him plainly; so I baited a large shark hook with a haddock and dropped it overboard. In a moment he swallowed it. Wild with excitement I rushed to the forecastle and shouted, "I have him."

The crew tumbled on deck to see what I did have, at once saw it was a shark, and proceeded to haul him up, my brother William standing by with the lance ready to kill him. To the surprise of all, the fish rolled the line round him, so that he came up tail first and could not be lanced for fear of cutting the line. He would hit hard enough blows on the side of the schooner to shake her, and in his struggles hit Eben Willard a blow on the face that knocked him down. Meanwhile my father talked strong language to me, and forbade my shark-fishing in future. "There's no sleeping where that boy is," he said.

THE WILLARD HOMESTEAD.

1813.

But after a time the shark turned, came up head first, and was easily killed by the lance. All hands then hoisted the monster on deck, when he was found to be fifteen feet in length and with jaws large enough to swallow a man whole. When the liver was taken out it filled a barrel and a half. Then father felt better, but said to me, "Ben, don't you ever put that hook out for shark again." I was always good to mind, and obeyed orders; but somehow I was continually getting into mischief before I knew it, though I never fished for shark again while on the "Martha Washington."

A MAMMOTH COD.—Later in the season we went on to the fishing ground called "Mistaken Ground," a good place for fish when the herring come on the coast. During the first day whales came and herring were schooling thick. You could see whales in all directions. One came up and rubbed so hard against the schooner as to careen her some. The monster was longer than the vessel. Being frightened I ran to the other side, when my father told me to pump some bilge water out. This I did, and the whale left in a hurry, but soon came up in the midst of a large school of herring, swallowing what must have been four or five barrels of them. But he was a good whale for us, for he drove as many more barrels into our nets, giving us plenty of bait next day when we fell in with numerous cod.

Three boats left the schooner next morning and returned before ten o'clock full of large cod. By two in the afternoon they returned with three more loads, my brother William stringing his painter (the line that tows the boat) with big fish. After dinner, which, being the boy, I had to get, the crew dressed and split the cod for salting and put them in the hold. After dinner I put out two lines in forty-five fathoms of water, and presently felt something big and strong pulling at one of them. It struggled nobly, while the crew looked on laughingly and shouted, "Tug, away, Bennie; you'll soon get him." They thought I was fast to one of those deep water skates, as large as a barn door and with three or four tails. The more I tugged the more they made fun of me. But I could say nothing. The boy on a vessel, as is well known, has to take all manner of insults and still keep cool. It is pretty hard work sometimes. At last I could see large bubbles of air and two big cod-fish on my line, so shouted to the crew to jump for their gaffs. Mr. William Jones, who was nearest the rail splitting fish, looked over and sang out so loud that all the crew sprang from their work to the side. The two fish were soon hauled on deck. It was estimated that the biggest one was good for 130 pounds, and it proved to weigh 75 pounds when dried. It was said to be the largest cod-fish ever landed on House Island, and the spots on it were as big as silver dollars. I think Mr. Alpha Sterling will remember that cod. It was the talk for many a day. In those days halibut were plenty. Saturday was the day to land fish at House Island. My father understood the movements of the fish well, and every week he went farther east, where the whales and herring were schooling the thickest. The third and last trip was made southeast from Monhegan Island, some twenty miles distant. In four or five days we filled the schooner three times. Every night the nets would fill with herring. After this three or four weeks were spent in cod-fishing. Then the schooner was fitted and painted, to fish for mackerel. In those days hook fishing was profitable, and good wages were made by the crews.

MY FIRST TRIP TO THE BANKS.—In 1843, or about that date, when I was fifteen years old, father saw a Cape Ann schooner come into Portland from Georges Bank with a large fare of halibut. So he fitted his schooner out for a trip himself, with sails and rigging about new, plenty of hemp cable, and an ice-pen holding two or three tons, on which was plenty of fresh bait. He took a supply of heavy leads to use in strong tides. Some of the crew felt a little shaky, as bad reports had been received of the loss of fishing vessels. However, as it was the best time of year for the trip, they concluded to make the venture. It took nearly three days with light winds to reach the north part of the Banks; and, just at that time, the wind changed to southeast, blowing a strong gale that lasted all one night; then it shifted to south and blew harder until it died out and a thick fog came. The sea was running mountains high, and it seemed at times the vessel would roll over. I was seasick, as I always was in rough weather. After four days of this sort of thing the sea went down, and I felt like getting on deck.

HOW I LOST MY BLACK STOCKINGS.—When I got out of my berth Mr. William Jones went for my feet, roughly hauled my stockings off, and threw them overboard, getting me another pair in their place. When I asked him what he did that for, he solemnly said: "Bennie, don't you ever wear black stockings on board this vessel again. We have had all this bad luck by your black stockings." This incident goes to show how superstitious sailors are. At times they will nail horseshoes on the heel of the bowsprit to keep the witches away from the vessel.

This was the first and last trip to Georges Banks.

The schooner was then headed for Jefferies Bank, where a good fare was got; and then back home; which all hands were glad enough to reach alive and well, and better satisfied for the future to stay on inner fishing grounds, where harbor could be made when heavy storms came on. But wasn't I seasick!

WHEN LOBSTERS WERE PLENTY. — About 1844 father sold the "Martha Washington" and built a cheap house for summer at Alewive Cove, Cape Elizabeth, to live in while he carried on fishing and lobstering. In those days lobsters were large and plenty, and a sloop smack, whose captain's name was Marston, came from Boston for them regularly. Cod-fish were also plenty near the coves and points, as they would follow the alewives to the brook leading up to the big pond on the cape, where they went to spawn. Millions went there for years, and if the brook were opened up for the alewives now, it would be worth thousands of dollars to the fishermen of Cape Elizabeth.

About this time father had a large Hampton boat built for me, of which I felt very proud; for she was big and safe. She was not so fast as some of my neighbors' boats; but I made up for that by rising early and reaching the grounds by daylight. There was fine fighting to get the best berths on White Head Ground and Drunken Ledge, as there seemed to be boiling springs at the bottom, where the fish went for fresh water. At a short distance from those places no fish could be caught. I have known but one man, in all my life, who could see for long distances, and make out flags on ships, as I could. This man was Mr. George Leavitt, of Willard, Cape Elizabeth. He is still living, and with eye-sight as good as ever — as indeed mine is, for that matter. When Mr. Leavitt and I were on those grounds, waiting to see our local marks, we would both get them at the same moment, and both killicks go down at the same time. It was then thought mean for one boat to anchor close to another engaged in catching fish; but if the two anchored at the same time it was all right. For bait we used clams until the porgies and herring came.

CHAPTER II.

THE HARBOR IN A FOG. — OLD TIME HOSPITALITY ON THE CAPE. — MY FIRST CHEW OF TOBACCO. — AN ANCIENT SCHOOL-HOUSE. — HOW FISHERMEN CAME TO USE COMPASSES. — THE HARM DONE TO HOOK FISHING BY SEINES AND SEALS.

IN foggy weather it is an easy thing to lose one's way on the water, even in our sheltered harbor. The following is a case in point: One day, late in the afternoon, as I was coming from Green Island and making for White Head, I saw a pleasure boat, filled with men, women, and children, heading out to sea. Knowing they must have lost their way I hailed them, and in reply was told they were going to Portland. Great was their surprise when told that they had mistaken their direction. I gave them a line and towed them to port. As we passed the Spindle, their astonishment was boundless at discovering that they had gone out by White Head, when they thought they were making good way to Portland; and in their gratitude, when landed at Commercial Wharf, they offered to pay me anything that might be asked.

In those days many boats were let for sailing parties; and I have often wondered that drowning accidents were so few, as many of the excursionists slaked their thirst with something stronger than water. Most of the fishermen would "fill up" Saturday and Sunday, though keeping sober on other days, when at their work. There were exceptions though. One day Mr. Some One ran ashore on Bangs Island (now called Cushing's) after imbibing too freely, and had to be hauled off by the fishermen from the cove. At another time another Mr. Somebody, who was careful not to set any sail when in drink, but trusted to his oars, rowed ashore at ebb-tide, where he remained for some time, the spectators amusing themselves at his expense. But I do not now remember of any fatal accidents happening to men in drink.

There was more hospitality in those times than now. When the fishermen went to Richmond's Island, they would spend the night in the barn on the hay. Mr. Jordan was always good to them, and did not call them tramps, as is the custom nowadays. The Cape Elizabeth fishermen themselves are kind-hearted and free-handed, ready to divide the last loaf with their neighbors if in need. Often, when a boy, I have heard my parents say that some family was in need. As soon as the news was noised about, the neighbors would go there with their arms full, and the next day a load of wood would be dropped at the door. No one had heard of "pound parties" then, to which each one carries a pound of something, and all stay half the night and eat the whole up.

My First Chew of Tobacco.—My first, and last, cud of tobacco was chewed while going to school. Washington Loveitt, Isaac Cobb, and myself mustered two cents apiece and bought a plug of pigtail twist. It was divided fairly, and we stowed a quid in our cheeks. All went merrily while we were in the open air, and we thought we were men indeed; but somehow the school-house seemed uncommonly warm. I began to sweat freely, and on looking at Cobb found he was getting white, while his hair was steaming. Pretty soon he asked leave to go and get a drink of water. About the time he got back to his seat I began to think a little water would be good for me. Before I got through, Loveitt started for the water pail, and Cobb asked to go out. I followed with Loveitt at my heels. Three sicker boys were never seen. We were absent so long that Mr. Enos Dyer, the school-master, suspected something and started in search of us. He at once saw the trouble, advised us never to chew again (advice which I have followed to this day), and told us to go home. This we were glad to do, but our hats were in the school-house. As Loveitt had the best legs, he brought our hats out; still, we could not walk without staggering, and so crawled on our hands and knees over the stone-wall, where we lay until school was out and the children gone. Then I went home and stole to bed without my supper. There my mother found me, sick, as she supposed, with a headache, and and bound my head up with burdock leaves steeped in vinegar. I have never taken a piece of tobacco into my mouth from that day to this. Of my companions, Mr. Loveitt is still living at Cape Elizabeth, and Mr. Cobb is gone.

AN OLD-TIME SCHOOL-HOUSE.—Sixty years ago school-houses were far different from those we build now. The one in our district, where I attended, was situated below the Danforth Hill, near the brook, on the shore road to Portland Light, a mile or more from Simonton's Cove. It was but one story, low-studded, narrow, and long like a ten-pin alley, and set end to the road. The long wood stove would take in uncut cord wood, and the funnel ran the whole length of the building it was supposed to heat; but in northeast snow-storms the snow would blow in round the windows, and those of us lucky enough to have overcoats were glad to use them, so bitter was the cold. We had a very nice book to take the place of grammar, a Robert B. Thomas Almanac. This we studied every night before going to bed, to see if the tide was fair at one o'clock in the morning, so that we could row to the fishing grounds. The master gave us Saturday afternoons for play, but that did not suit the big boys, so they would fill the funnel Saturday morning with juniper bushes and smoke everybody out. The result would be the adjournment of school until Monday, so that the funnel might be cleaned out. Then the big boys would start for the rabbit swamp and spend the rest of the day hunting.

How Fishermen Came To Use the Compass.—At that time no compasses were used by the fishermen. They all went to any shoal they wished, steering by the sea. In thick fog a swell would roll in from the ocean, and the lead was used when near the shoal. Compasses were not employed till some of the boats got lost in a snow-storm coming home from White Head Grounds, being misled by the changing off wind and no land in sight. (You cannot run by the sea in a snow-storm; as the wind changes you will steer by that). One or two of the boats made Stratton Island, and some Richmond Island, but all got into good harbors before night fell, where they remained until the storm was over. Meanwhile much anxiety was felt at home for their safety, and thereafter they were persuaded to take compasses.

About 1846 I took Mr. James Cobb into company. In early spring we went in the large boat, but later on used both. Cobb was smart and prompt, and the quickest man to wake from sound sleep I ever knew. If you spoke to him in a moderate tone of voice, ten feet away, he would spring up at once. The second year we were together we heard, about the last of June, that mackerel were plenty off Cape Ann and coming east in large schools; so I fitted the large boat and started to meet them off Boon Island, knowing that I could put into Portsmouth or old York for harbor, in case of a storm. Mr. Cobb took the small boat to fish on Cod Ledge; we both had good luck, and came back to Portland loaded with cod and mackerel, for which we got a fair price, clearing about forty dollars apiece —which came in very handy, for the Fourth of July was close at hand. My mackerel usually went to Mr. John Loveitt, for he always did the right thing by the fishermen.

SEINES AND SEALS.—In those days all the boats made money fast, but after a time so many were brought in that prices went down. Now a mackerel is rarely caught with the hook. What with seining on the outside and seals on the inside, where mackerel used to go and spawn, and where boats in August and September could catch from fifty to three hundred pounds anywhere in Casco Bay, real old-fashioned fishing is about ruined; but drive the seals out of the bay and the mackerel will come again. The seals are now so numerous that they go to sea for food. I have seen them ten miles out in summer, the ledges fairly swarming with them, basking in the sun.

As for seining, the porgy steamers with their seines have driven the fish off the coast. The last time the porgies came back they had been absent twelve years. When they are on the coast and in the bays, fish of all kinds come into the shoal water, and the fishermen by setting nets get all the bait they want. If all seining were to be stopped for a reasonable time, so as to give the fish a chance to breed and not frighten them away, the shore fishermen could once again get a good living by hook fishing. But they never can till then.

I think 1848 was the best year I ever saw for the fishermen in boats. At the Hue and Cry Shoal Mr. Cobb and myself got from daylight to noon something over 1,400 pounds of mackerel. All the other boats did as well, and some of them better. We often saw fifteen or twenty boats in one string. The mackerel came along shore in large schools, and were found in Casco Bay, Harpswell Bay, New Meadows, and around shoals everywhere. I have seen great schools inside of Bangs Island. Now the seining, south in the spring, has driven the large body of them outside of Nantucket Shoals to the northern part of the Gulf Stream and to Nova Scotia waters. Had the seine never been used, our coast would be good to-day for hook fishing, and far better for all classes of fishermen.

Trawl fishing, too, has hurt cod trade; for it catches up the mother fish that rarely bites at hand lines. When I was young the bank fishermen would come home with flags flying and a full cargo, and fill the flakes at House Island. I have rowed many merchants to this island to buy fish. To-day the flakes are down and the island looks desolate.

CHAPTER III.

THE LOSS OF THE PLEASURE BOAT "LEO" IN CASCO BAY. — DEATH BY DROWNING OF A WOMAN AND EIGHT CHILDREN. — LIVING ON CRACKER CRUMBS IN THE BAY OF FUNDY. WHIMSICAL ADVENTURE NEAR BIDDEFORD POOL. — A PERILOUS PASSAGE FROM PHILADELPHIA TO PORTLAND.

THE sad accident to the pleasure boat "Leo," near Hog Island Ledge, by which nine lives were lost, is not yet forgotten by the older people of Portland. It was on the 22d of July, 1848, that I passed the boat as she was going down the harbor, and noted that she had two sails up, while one was all a careful man would like to carry; but took no further thought, having seen many pleasure boats loaded with passengers in the hands of men unaccustomed to handle them in a strong wind. The wind was then blowing hard from the southwest.

When the pleasure boat "Favorite" came home in the evening she reported seeing a boat suddenly disappear near Hog Island Ledge. This aroused anxiety for the "Leo," and Mr. Edward Harlow, her owner, started for the ledge. When near it he heard a man crying for help, and soon found Mr. William Smith clinging to the mast-head of the sunken boat and nearly dead from exhaustion. This was at eleven o'clock in the night. It seeemed that the "Leo" upset about eight o'clock. All the passengers except Mr. Smith, including his wife and four children and the four children of Mr. and Mrs. John Whyley, were drowned. The man in charge of the boat, a sailor, named Stephenson, swam to the ledge, from which he was taken off by the rescuing party. When the news of the accident spread, all the fishermen of the vicinity turned out with hooks and grapples to recover the bodies; but the eel-grass was long and got tangled in the hooks, so that three of the children, one belonging to the Whyley family, were never found. The body of Mrs. Smith was found floating several days later, and I grappled that of her son, a boy about six years old. When the "Leo" was raised (her mast was some four feet out of water, at low tide) it was seen that the fore sheet had been made fast — a fact showing bad management.

I BECOME MY OWN MAN. — In the fall of 1848, when I was twenty years old, my father kindly gave me one year, and much to my pleasure I became my own man.

The summer of 1849 was good for fishing at Simonton's Cove, and Mr. Cobb and myself made it a profitable season. The next summer I shipped as mate with my brother, E. G. Willard, in the schooner "Jerome," a vessel of 106 tons register and capable of carrying 150 tons of coal; this being about the usual size of coasters at that date. While mate of this vessel I saw some hard service; particularly on a voyage to the Bay of Fundy, where I passed gloomy hours on an uninhabited island with nothing to eat but cracker crumbs, and mighty few of them. We were from Portland, bound for Calais, and, though the morning was fine at the hour of sailing, the schooner ran into a fog before we had gone far — fog which lasted two days without any signs of lifting. On the afternoon of the second day we struck shoal water and let go the anchor. As we thought we could hear the surf a short distance to the north, the yawl boat was lowered and my brother and I jumped into her, leaving Mr. John F. Loveitt and Talbert, the cook, on board. We put off into the thick fog, but could find nothing. Before long the tide and wind changed against us, darkness came on, and in spite of all our efforts we steadily drifted away from the ship. For a time we could hear the horn, and after that a gun. (Subsequently we learned that Loveitt kept on firing the gun until his powder gave out.) After rowing five or six hours we had to give it up and drift wherever the strong wind and tide would carry us. It was a long and dark night, and as we had no oil clothes or extra coats we suffered severely from the cold and wet.

About daylight we heard the surf beating on the rocks, and let the lead go down, but found no bottom. Presently we saw the breakers and both braced up to keep the boat clear of them. As it grew lighter we saw a small island with high banks and heavily wooded. There we landed, shivering with cold and wet to the skin. Though we stayed ashore a long time, no signs of life could be seen. After a time we caught a glimpse of a larger island, and setting off for that, had the good fortune to find an English pilot boat laying there. Going on board, we were heartily welcomed by the crew, who gathered about, eager to hear our story. The first thing they offered us was rum, which, as neither of us had ever tasted liquor, we declined — to their utter amazement. They had run short of provisions, but managed to get some coffee and food for us, which we devoured eagerly. It was little enough, but nearly all they had, though rum was plenty.

Our anxiety for the "Jerome" was so great that

as soon as we were warmed and a bit rested we engaged a pilot to set out in search of her. He thought she must be anchored at Seal Island Rips, and that the sound we took for the surf was the high tide on the rips; so he started for there, but was baffled by the heavy winds and came back to his starting point. Then my brother and I took the yawl boat and went ashore to find something to eat. All we found was an empty building fastened up tightly, and in order to enter it we had to unscrew the hinges from the door. Nothing was there but a few hard bread crumbs in the bottom of a barrel. These tasted sweet and good, but went only a little way toward satisfying our hunger. We replaced the hinges, and would have left money for food had we found anything to eat.

Pulling back to the ship we passed the night there, but could not sleep much as our minds were on the "Jerome" and the two men left alone with her. We well knew that she could not ride long in that high wind and sea; so the next morning the pilot boat got under way and started on her search. As nothing could be seen of the missing vessel I asked to be landed at Eastport, where we might get news of her. So we made for that harbor, and to our great joy came across the "Jerome" making for the same shelter. Their relief was as great as ours, for they had almost given us up for lost. It seems that the schooner went adrift; but they were fortunate enough to reach the lee of Libby Island, where they anchored until the wind abated. After paying the pilot and stocking him up with provisions, the first thing my brother and I did was to make for the cabin double quick and eat a good dinner, the first we had had for two days. Food never tasted so good to me before.

It seems that the next day after my brother and I left the "Jerome" at anchor at Seal Island Rips she struck a drift in a high wind and fog. Mr. Loveitt and the cook reefed the sails, set them, and slipped the chain; loosing the small anchor and chain and steering northwest until they made breakers. They tacked off, then tacked back. In tacking back the schooner had gone to the leeward, with the strong tide, enough to come under the lee of Libby Island into smooth water, where she anchored with the big anchor. The next day the wind was west and the fog clearing. Loveitt saw three fishermen lobstering, put his flag in the rigging, called them aboard, and made a trade with them to pilot and help get the vessel to Eastport. While on the way we boarded her with the pilot boat. The fishermen were paid in money, and the pilot in ship stores. Then the pilot took the fishermen back home. Our yawl boat was hoisted up and the vessel kept off for Calais, where we loaded a cargo of laths for Philadelphia. Before we finally got out of the Bay of Fundy the fog shut in again and followed us to Cape Cod. The passage out was good, as we had favorable winds to the Capes of Delaware. We all felt good to get away from Fundy alive. I have not been there since, and have no desire to go again; getting all I wanted and more than I bargained for that time.

WRECKED IN SACO RIVER.—From Philadelphia we took a cargo of coal to Saco, Maine, and on arriving at Biddeford Pool Captain Tappen was engaged as pilot. Going up the Saco River the schooner ran ashore in the mud; and a pleasure steamboat called "The Belle" was employed to pull her off and tow her up to town. While discharging cargo, the "Belle" advertised to give a moonlight sail down the river and a dance at the ferry. Mr. Loveitt and I invited some lady friends to go. On the return, about midnight, we met with a ludicrous adventure. The boat ran on to a little island in the darkness near the Narrows, and stove a hole in the bottom. As she began to fill fast, the fires were drawn, the steam blown out, and the gangway plank run out towards the island. We men had to take the lady passengers ashore in our arms through three feet of water. A lame man on board offered Mr. Loveitt and me five dollars to "tote" him to land, and we promised to do it for nothing as soon as the ladies were looked out for; but he would not wait, and was soon on the shoulders of two other men, one of whom slipped and dumped him into the stream. Just as all had got ashore safely, some dories came up and were sent to town for transportation. Meanwhile, we made a fire on the island, and passed the time pleasantly until the boats could carry us across the river to the Saco side, where teams were in readiness to take us to town, which we reached about sunrise. Saco River was certainly the last place in which I ever expected to be wrecked.

A PERILOUS NOVEMBER PASSAGE.—The roughest passage I ever had while mate of the "Jerome" was from Philadelphia to Portland, with a cargo of coal, in November, 1850. We had favorable winds until off Chatham Light, when threatening weather set in and lasted until we reached port. The wind got round to the east and made a heavy sea fast. As it began to blow more heavily we shortened sail, keeping just enough canvas spread to get by the high land of Cape Cod. After passing Peaked Hill Bar the schooner was hove to under three-reefed mainsail for a dead drift into Boston Bay. Before morning the sea boarded her, stove the galley doors down, and washed everything out but the stove. The gale lasted until nine o'clock in the forenoon, and a few hours after we struck a snow-squall and were obliged to throw our deck load of coal overboard to lighten the vessel. The sea ran high and came tumbling on deck, and some of the waist-boards had to be knocked off to let the water out quickly.

My brother carried sail as long as it could be done safely, but finally had to heave to. It began to look like a close shave, and I lashed some kegs for life preservers in case we were driven ashore. I kept sounding with a deep-sea line, and about midnight found bottom. At this moment my hands grew so numb that I lost the line. A new one was hastily improvised by unreefing the pennant halyards from the main topmast, and the next sounding showed no shoaler water. Then we all began to feel a little easier. When daylight came the snow cleared away, and we ran up under the lee of Chatham, and anchored with our big anchor weighing over a thousand pounds. There we lay for two days, as a big sea was rolling round the cape.

When the wind changed to the west and the sea went down we headed for Portland, having favorable winds and fair weather until we got about half-way between Cape Cod and Cape Elizabeth. Then another snow-squall struck us, and we had a succession of them the rest of the voyage, until near Cape Elizabeth lights. Then the squalls ceased and we made Portland. When we arrived there our decks looked as if they had been holy-stoned with sand for a week.

CHAPTER IV.

IN WHICH I BECOME A SHIP-OWNER. — THE GREAT APRIL GALE OF 1851. — RIDING IT OUT IN LITTLE EGG HARBOR. — THE RACE FROM PHILADELPHIA TO PORTLAND. — FORSAKING SEA FOR LAND SERVICE.

IN the winter of 1851 I bought a quarter interest in the "Jerome," and took charge of her, having very good luck in making quick trips between Portland and Philadelphia; nor did my good fortune desert me in the great April gale of that year, when so many vessels were lost and lives sacrificed. Sailing from Philadelphia for New York, on the 18th of that month, I had a quick run to ten miles north of Barnegat Light. Four hours more would have carried me to Sandy Hook; but the wind sprang up from the northeast, the weather thickened, and there was every indication of a strong gale; so I ran back off Little Egg Harbor. Something told me to put in there, though all I had to go by was courses from buoys, jotted down on a piece of paper and given to me by a New Jersey captain.

I ran for the first buoy, but before getting to it saw two men in a boat beckoning for me to luff. I did so, and presently the boat pulled alongside. The men proved to be pilots who told me that the way I was taking would carry the vessel on to a nine-feet shoal. On quoting the New Jersey captain's directions, they said that would be all right in ordinary times, but the ice had changed the buoy some distance to the southwest, and the government had not had time to move it back.

MINOT'S LEDGE LIGHT-HOUSE.

We lay at Little Egg Harbor for three days, waiting for the heavy swell to go down; for the gale was long and terrific and the tide, the highest known for years, covering the low lands inside the sea banks for many miles. While there I feasted on excellent codfish, which they kept alive as the Maine smacks do lobsters in their wells. The rest of the voyage was uneventful, though we passed many wrecks; and, on arriving in New York, the first thing I saw in the newspapers was an account of that memorable and destructive storm which washed down Minot's Ledge Light-house, drowned the keepers, and spread devastation all along that part of the coast. I am satisfied that if I had not run into Little Egg Harbor I should have been lost, for my vessel could not live fifteen hours in that gale—though what impulse drove me to my determination I cannot tell to this day. Minot's Ledge Light-house (of which an excellent illustration is given on page 37) was on a rock about twenty miles from Boston, built of solid iron piles, sixty feet high and ten inches in diameter. The fury of a gale sufficient to overthrow it can scarcely be imagined.

The most of my coal freights from Philadelphia to Portland were consigned to Messrs. Charles and Abel Baker, who kept a coal yard on Richardson's Wharf. They were both honest gentlemen to deal with. I made many quick trips, arriving ahead of the bill of lading on one of them. On receiving the bill Mr. Abel Baker at once went to an insurance officer and paid $40 for insuring the cargo. Great was his astonishment on returning to find me sitting in his office and my vessel hauling up to his coal shed. At that time freights in winter and spring were $3.00 to $3.50 a ton, and in summer about $1.50 to $1.75.

A Race Up the North Coast.—In 1851 my brother, E. G. Willard, built a centreboard schooner in Philadelphia, which carried about 240 tons of coal. She was so large it was very difficult to get a full cargo unless we took two or three different sizes of coal. When his vessel was nearly ready to be launched she was named the "E. G. Willard," and I took his sails, rigging, and fittings out there in the "Jerome" on my next trip. She was rigged and already to go up river to Bristol, twenty miles above Philadelphia, to load coal for Portland, for three round trips and a half. It was sharp racing.

I will cite the first passage from Bristol to Portland. Both vessels loaded at one time, shoved off from the coal docks about 6 P. M., calm and first ebb-tide. We drifted down river all that tide, and anchored for the next ebb-tide. The next day the wind was southwest, both vessels beating down river with the tide, and both keeping near together until we got down to Chester. Then he put his centreboard down and gained away from me fast, and when I got down to Reedy Island he was nearly hull down. At that time we took a fearful squall from the northwest with thunder, lightning, and rain. I ran under short sail down to Bomby Hook and anchored. As the night was very dark and the wind blowing hard, I did not think it safe to run down the bay. At that time I thought E. G. was far enough ahead to make Cross Ledge light ship and keep on going down the bay. At two next morning the anchor was hove up and we started down the bay. At daylight in the morning I was within a mile of E. G. He was getting under way, having anchored there, as it was thick weather and shoal water. When half-way down the bay he ran for Cape

May. My vessel drawing twelve feet, I had to run down the ship channel and out round the over falls. When out there he was hull down ahead. The next day the wind changed from northwest to south. When back of Long Island the fog shut in, and there was about a six or seven knot breeze. I shaped my course for Gay Head. The next morning between three and four I hove to to wait for daylight. When morning came we squared away for Vineyard Sound, the fog still holding thick, and our horn blowing at short intervals. We could hear other horns in most any direction, but could see no vessels. When getting near the Vineyard both anchors were got in readiness; one man was sent to the foremast head to look over the fog, if possible, and see land, one man set to heaving the lead on the starboard quarter. By letting out fifteen or twenty fathoms of line the sheets were hauled aft, so as to luff quick if needed. After we run our time up in about twenty or thirty minutes, the lookout forward reported breakers on the port bow. I luffed quick. On luffing I could see, under the main boom, breakers a hundred yards off. At that time there were by the lead line eight to nine fathoms. The next sounding there was no bottom at fifteen to twenty fathoms. The vessel was kept off on her course again, and run sometime, when breakers were sighted again on her port bow. I luffed some and run parallel with the breakers. Shortly the fog lifted a little, and I saw the timbers of an old wreck that I had seen several times before, and I knew them. It was a short distance southerly of Quick's Hole.

Then I shaped my course for the middle ground, got soundings, and sheered off and on, until we got up to West Chop. With about a four knot breeze and wind south southwest we went up to West Chop, made Spar Buoy, and run down the sound the usual course. The fog was very thick. When some three or four miles to the eastward of East Chop the wind died out, there was a head tide, and we anchored. I went below to get some rest, leaving orders to call me when there was wind enough to stem tide. When I had been below an hour or an hour and a half I was called. I came on deck and got under way, heading down the sound, with all the light sails put on. The fog was very thick and wet, with about three knot breeze, the fog-horn still blowing at short intervals. After a long time running the lookout reported a light right ahead. I hove the wheel hard up at once. As the vessel swung off quickly I saw the light between the foremast and fore rigging, and when the light got by the fore rigging, I steadied the wheel. As we were getting close upon the light, it proved to be the light ship with no bell ringing.

We cleared the light ship side from about eight to ten feet. I sang out to him in strong language, and asked him why he did not ring his bell. His answer was: "What are you running such a night as this is for?"

I told him there were fifty vessels astern of me and I guess he thought so, for I heard the bell ringing until I got by Sandy Point. It being too thick to run for Pollock Rip light ship, I ran out Ship Channel, around the great round shoal. When in deep water off the shoals the gaff topsails were clued up, the main peak dipped and jibed over and hoisted up, and the gaff topsail set, running the course up the back side of Cape Cod for Portland. When up between Chatham and Nosset, we run out of the fog, and a fresh, warm breeze came off from the sand hills, and, behold, there was the "E. G." about a mile ahead. I run up my burgee and in a short time he run up his in answer.

When passing Nosset Light we shaped course for Cape Elizabeth. When some fifteen miles north of Cape Cod, it commenced a southerly gale with rain, and all the light sails had to be taken in; single reef in the mainsail, the foresail jib, and flying jib. As it would be dark before I could get to Cape Elizabeth by running a straight course, I hauled to some to make the land to the westward of Wood Island before dark. I could see at that time about a half-mile before making the land. I could see a fishing schooner ahead and hove to, heading off shore under reef foresail. I kept off some to speak him, and when near him I was about to ask him how Wood Island bore; but before I could speak he asked me how Portland Light bore. I told him how I judged Cape Elizabeth to bear, and I asked him if he had seen land. By this time we were too far by to hear him; but he pointed his hand in shore as though he had seen land. After passing him he kept off to follow us. We were keeping a sharp lookout at the time as we thought we were nearing the shore, and one man was placed to the mainpeak halyards, ready to dip peak for wearing. In a short time surf was seen on shore. We at once wore around with main peak hoisted up, and kept on running parallel with the surf. We could see at the time about half a mile distant, and when opposite Wood Island Light they were just lighting it. The fishing schooner was on the starboard quarter. As I saw he was going to follow I hung a lantern on the starboard davit and run for the back side of Richmond Island. The flying jib was hauled down and furled. We run on that course until breakers were seen on the port bow. The helm was put hard down at once. When the vessel came to, to be in the trough of the sea, the vessel shipped a great deal of water amidships. All hands were on the main sheet hauling in to keep it from slatting in the wind. The water soon ran off from the deck. The breakers that I saw we supposed to be Adam's Head on the back side of Richmond Island. I let her jog off shore easy until I could steer a straight course for the back side of Cape Elizabeth and clear Watts Ledge. When I luffed from Adam's Head the fishing schooner came near running into mine. In a few minutes I kept off for the back side of Cape Elizabeth.

The mate advised me to haul off shore for the night. I told him I was going to Portland, that there was bold water near the Cape; I had caught cunners off from every foot of it, and it was safe to go within a schooner's length of the shore. I ran until I thought we ought to see something. I began to think we were running too wide off to see shore or lights; but in a few minutes the lookout reported breakers broad off the port bow. I luffed a couple of points and run by the breakers. When opposite the Cape lights I could just see them through the mist and fog. I run until I judged I was by Broad Cove Rock and Trundy's Reef Shoal.

Then I jibed over, to run for Portland Head. The wind dying away some, the fog and mist seemed to be thicker. As I neared up to Portland Head I could hear the rote on shore to the south of it. I kept off some and the lookout reported a light right ahead. I kept off at once and found it to be Portland Head Light, and passed in by very near the Point.

Then all sail was put on. When inside of Ship

Cove we run out of the fog. It was all clear in the harbor and I could see coasters' lights anchored in Hog Island Roads. Then the fisherman put all sail on and passed me very quickly, thanking me, and said it was well done. When I was inside Spring Point Buoy the wind died out, a head tide set in, and I anchored. I lowered the boat and took two men and rowed to Commercial Wharf. Then I started for the *Argus* office. I found my way up the back stairs where the boys were setting type, and reported the arrival of the schooner "Jerome," Willard, from Philadelphia. In the morning the papers had "E. G. Willard," Willard, and "Jerome," Willard, from Philadelphia, reported for three round trips and a half. Both vessels were reported the same day arriving and clearing at Philadelphia and Portland.

The next day, on seeing E. G., I found he made, in coming into the Vineyard, Nymshebite, north of Gay Head; he sounding up on the north of Vineyard Island and keeping on sounding until he got up to the middle ground; sounding, off and on, on the south side of the middle ground up to West Chop. When some distance below East Chop he anchored for some two hours. When it breezed up he got under way, running out over the shoals in Ship Channel. When off Nosset, it being clear weather, he run straight for Cape Elizabeth. When nearing the Cape the first thing sighted was Alden's Rock Buoy, close to the bow, just giving him time to keep off to clear the shoals. When up to Portland Light they were just lighting it.

At that time the schooner "Jerome" was at Wood Island Light. That shows the difference of sailing in one day.

How I Left the Coasting Trade.—In the

summer of 1853 I was taken sick with fever and ague, and I got Capt. Thomas Bibber to handle the schooner for one or two trips. While he was running her I suddenly made up my mind one night that I would try and get my living ashore hereafter; so as soon as able I called on Jones and Hammond, my owners, stated my business, and said that I wanted to sell them my interest in the "Jerome." They wanted me to reconsider the matter, and offered to build me a larger vessel if I wanted it. But I told them my mind was made up for a change. Then they said that when I sold they wished me to sell their interest also; so on the next arrival of the schooner at Portland she was sold to Captain Potter, a colored man.

My Quickest and Slowest Coasting Trips.—Before leaving the account of my coasting trips, it may interest my readers to learn about the speediest and the slowest made while master of the "Jerome."

The quickest trip was from Philadelphia and return inside of ten days, with cargo each way.

The longest was twenty-eight days and return. January 12, 1853, at 4 P. M., I was towed down Portland Harbor by the steam tug "Tiger," the wind being northeast and a snow-storm coming on. Mr. George Dow was deck-hand on the "Tiger" at the time. Thinking that it would be a long storm I ran southeast instead of south for Cape Cod, so as to be to the windward if necessary to go out the South Channel. The next morning at daylight a high sea broke into the jib, and tore it out of the bolt rope. We ran under short sail the whole day, and at night hove to in South Channel, the sea running too high to send. In the morning, about seven, we parted both bobstays and came near losing our masts over the stern.

We immediately got a stay from the mainmast head to the windlass, hoisted the two-reef foresail, kept off for scudding, and furled the three-reef mainsail. Mr. Bishop Fuller, of Portland, was mate with me. He put a rope around his body, and, attended by the crew, fished up the bobstays to put on tackles, which was a very dangerous and risky job. He was wet to the skin. We kept on scudding until well by South Shoal. Then we hauled up for Long Island, hoping to get near it before the wind changed to the northwest. The gale and snow lasted for forty-eight hours, and wrecked several vessels on Cape Cod, and along the Jersey shore from Sandy Hook to Barnegat.

When we got within thirty miles of Long Island the wind came off northwest with snow-squalls and blowing a heavy gale. We furled head sails and hove to under three-reef mainsail for a dead drift. The schooner was making good weather and was perfectly tight. The wake to the windward broke the heavy combers before they got to the vessel, and we only got light water from them.

We drifted in this gale almost six days before it abated. Then we had baffling winds for two or three days, with vapor. By this time we were a long distance out in the Gulf Stream. Then we had one calm day with the sun out bright, this being the only day for twenty-two that we got a sight of the sun. All this bad weather we had to cook in the cabin over a cylinder stove, and sit on the cabin floor to eat our meals. Then we took a southeast gale and rain storm; and I made good use of it by scudding for Cape May under two-reef foresail.

We arrived in Philadelphia after twenty-two days out from Portland; discharged the cargo in one day, and the sail-maker made me a new jib by working night and day, so that I got my load the next forenoon and my new jib in the afternoon, and bent it going down by Red Bank in a northeast snow-storm. At dark we came to anchor off from Chester. The next morning the weather was clear and the wind north, giving us fair wind down the river and bay. Then the wind came west and gave us fair wind all the way home in four days.

On arriving home I found that my folks had given me up as lost, as all the papers contained accounts of bad wrecks and big loss of life along the entire coast; and they reminded me that my brother Samuel, who sailed for Cuba in the new bark "Martha Anna," January 12, 1852, at 4 P.M.—just one year to a day and hour before I set sail—was never heard from. This coincidence aroused their fears for my safety.

If I had run for Cape Cod the first night I should have been on a lee shore, as the wind canted out east the next day. Being to the windward I could go out of the channel with all safety, as I was about twenty-five miles from Cape Cod and Nantucket Shoals. I am satisfied if I had run for Cape Cod the first night I should have been among the wrecks reported that memorable week.

CHAPTER V.

IN WHICH I BECOME A STEVEDORE AND SUBSEQUENTLY A PILOT.—TAKING THE ALLAN STEAMSHIPS INTO PORT.—PILOTING A BONDED VESSEL, AND THE TROUBLE IT BROUGHT.—HOW I WAS UNJUSTLY PUT IN JAIL, AND MY EXPERIENCES THERE.—AN APPEAL FOR LONG-DELAYED JUSTICE.—SOME AMUSING EXPERIENCES.

AFTER leaving the coasting trade I went into company with William Lowry in the stevedoring business, our first outfit being two horses with coal tubs, etc. We worked one horse on a double whip, taking out from 100 to 125 tons of coal a day. The yearly total that came to Portland was 11,000 tons. After two years the firm dissolved and I went into business for myself. At that time sugar and molasses were hoisted out with the old-fashioned winch. Two or three years later oxen were used, and then horses; my span being the first used for Chase & Sloan, the riggers. In those days riggers took out all cargoes of sugar and molasses. In 1856 I took Mr. Daniel Gould into company. We had a steam engine made in East Boston, set on wheels to haul around to the wharves and hoist coal and molasses. Gould attended to the shore business, and I started to piloting ships.

I BECOME A PILOT.—My first winter of piloting was in a pleasure boat, with a cuddy forward and no deck aft, owned by Capt. Charles Harford, whose services I hired for the winter. He was brought up a Newfoundland sealer, and could stand more cold weather than any man I ever knew. The Allan steamships, "North American," "Anglo Saxon," and "Indian," ran fortnightly that winter between Liverpool and Portland direct. I saw some rough weather and hard work during the season, and had my first, and last, experience in being hauled on board a steamship with the bowline. As I bumped against the sides the breath was nearly knocked out of my body. When I was hauled on board the steamship "North American" the ship rolled down and ducked me twice in the cold water before Chief Officer Eaton had men enough on the rope to haul me up. Finally two men mounted the rail to light up while the men on deck took in the slack. I shouted, "Are you going to keep me here all day?" Since then I have preferred some other way to reach a ship's deck. It was not until the winter piloting was over, and the boat on the beach, that I discovered a big seam about three feet long in her bottom, with only tarred canvas and sheet lead tacked over it. My hair stood on end. If I had known the condition she was in, I would not have ventured outside of Portland Light in her.

While out for one of these ships, the wind northwest, a gale, and cold, I stood out by White Head near night to see if there was any signal on the Observatory. I was under very short sail so as to go slow and not ice up. Shortly I saw a row boat coming towards me. When near I saw Capt. Smith Hadlock, of Peaks Island. I asked him what he was out there in the cold for, and he said, "What are you out here for?" I told him I was out there to see if there was any signal out on the Observatory, as I was looking for a steamship. He told me why he came was that he thought my boat was in a crippled condition and came to render his assistance if needed.

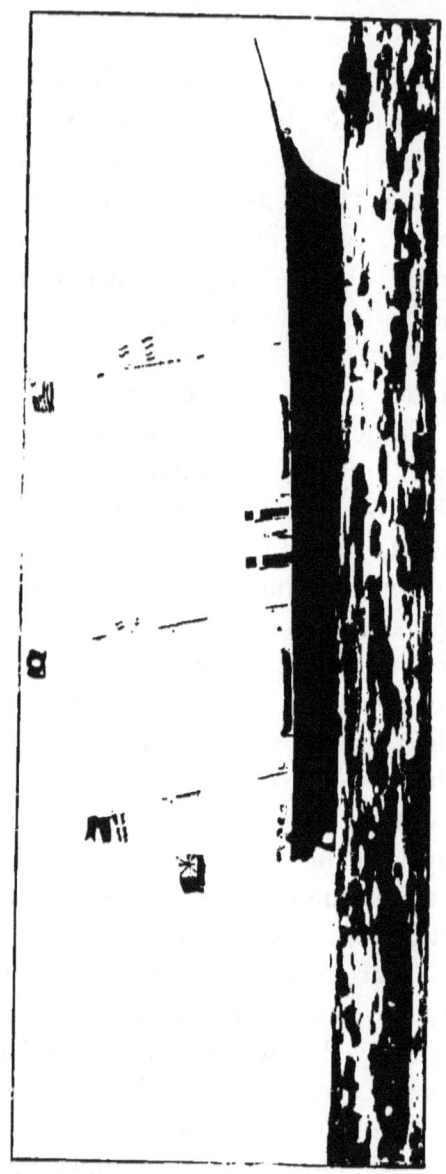
BRITISH STEAMSHIP "ANTELOPE," CAPTAIN JOHN SMITH.

My Trouble With a Bonded Steamship.—In the summer of 1857 I bought a schooner yacht named "The Alida," and fitted her for a pilot boat. Late in the summer of that year the British steamship, "Antelope," came to this port from Liverpool. Capt. David Jones came passenger, and piloted the ship into port, and when she went to sea I piloted her out. She came to Portland on a second trip and I piloted her in. She discharged and took in cargo. Before she left port a party of people from the Second Parish Church were invited to a dinner on board by the captain, who always appeared to be a very religious man. He told me that he wanted to go into the stream that afternoon as he had a permit from the United States Marshal. About five o'clock it was high water and I took her into the stream. The ship was attached on a former voyage for a coal debt of $1,000. Mr. John H. Cox, Jr., was ship keeper at the time. Captain Smith told me that he expected his agent would bond her.

After the tea-table was cleared, decanters and different kinds of liquors were brought on. I was invited to partake, but declined. The evening was spent waiting for orders, but no boat came. I told the captain I would retire as I had been broken of my rest the night before. He told the waiters to show me a room. On leaving the saloon I left Captain Smith, Mr. Cox, and several passengers there. About two o'clock the next morning the captain roused me and said, " A boat has been off, the ship is bonded, and you can take her to sea when you see fit." I was soon on the pilot bridge, and in two hours we were steaming out of the harbor. When near Portland Light I gave the captain a card marked, "S. E. by S. ten miles distance from Portland Head." This course I gave all captains on going out of the harbor. The captain then asked me where I would leave the ship. I told him a short distance outside Portland Light. He asked me then if my boat was big enough to take the keeper ashore. I told him it was, and he said if it was not he would lower a boat and set him ashore at Portland Head. Not seeing Mr. Cox since the night before, I supposed he went ashore when the boat came off. I asked the captain where the keeper was, and he said he was below asleep. I said, "Have him called at once, for I shall leave in a few minutes." When Mr. Cox came on the bridge he asked me how it was that the ship was going out. I told him what the captain said when he came to my state-room. He then asked me where the captain was and I said, "There he is on the forward part of the house."

Mr. Cox went to talk with him. While they were in conversation I rang the bell to stop the engine. The ship then was on her course. I left the bridge and went to the ship gangway to see to the lowering of my boat, and dropped astern to the ship ladder for leaving. I was in the boat some minutes before Mr. Cox came. While I was rowing him home, he said he could not see into it; that when he went on board his orders from Mr. Quimby were to stay there until he had written or verbal orders that the ship was clear.

He thought it was all right until he got home; but after seeing Mr. Quimby he found it was all wrong. I, as pilot, was indicted for aiding and abetting Captain Smith in taking the ship to sea, and put under bonds to appear at the June term of 1858. Mr. Edward Fox was my counsel. When the case came up for trial Mr. Fox said the case could be settled for $400. I told him that I took the ship out in good faith, and would not pay one dollar.

I Am Sentenced to Jail. — When Mr. Cox was on the stand in court, he stated that he repeatedly forbade Captain Willard to pilot the ship to sea. I say that statement was false. How could he repeatedly forbid Captain Willard piloting the ship to sea, when he was in his state-room asleep until called to leave the ship with the pilot?

My sentence by Judge Ware was sixty days in the county jail and $20 fine, imposed June 12, 1858. Mr. Adams, now in the firm of Rollins & Adams, was jail keeper at the time. When the officer took me to his office, he said he would put me in the debtor cell, the best room in jail, with some four or five men who were in there for debt. At this time Cox and Williams were in jail for murdering all the crew of the brig "Albion Cooper." After being in jail two or three days Mr. Quimby came to Mr. Adams and told him that if Captain Willard wanted the liberty of the yard he could have it; at the same time saying that the merchants were making a great deal of talk about the case. Mr. Adams came to my cell and told me that if I wished to have the liberty of the yard I could have it. I thanked him, and said that I did not wish to have any more liberty than those in the cell with me. The food was good, and plenty of it, but I had no use for it as my friends brought me enough for those in the cell with me. One day Capt. Thomas Libby, on arriving from Cuba, on his way home from his brig brought to my cell a market basket full of oranges, pine-apples, and a box of cigars. When in jail about seven days, Mr. Henry Goddard called to talk with me through the iron grates, and said to me that he had called on Mr. Quimby to know what he was going to do with Captain Willard when they moved the prisoners, as the old jail was about to be torn down. Quimby said, "Auburn with the other United States prisoners." Mr. Goddard replied that it lay with him to say whether Willard should go out to the work-house or to Auburn. If to the work-house his friends could go to see him, but if Quimby had fully made up his mind to send Willard to Auburn with Cox and Williams, the murderers, he could get a new bondsman before the sun went down that night. After some sharp talk Mr. Quimby decided that Willard could go to the work-house, and he then left his office and went to my cell to inform me of the fact.

SEVEN WEEKS IN THE WORK-HOUSE. — After spending ten days in the old jail, the county prisoners were transferred to the work-house, Cox and Williams, the murderers, being sent to Auburn. Mr. Adams told me I could step into the yard until he got the prisoners off, and he would take me out in his wagon. The prisoners were all moved in hacks. As Cox and Williams got into one they seemed to me the roughest looking men that I ever saw. On arriving at the work-house I was introduced to Mr. Richard Webster, the keeper, who told me to take a seat in the office and when he had fixed the prisoners he would attend to me. When he came back he invited me upstairs, showed me a large front room, nicely furnished, and said that I could have that one. I told him that one was too nice for a prisoner, and that I preferred a smaller one where I could learn to paint ships and flags. He showed me a smaller one, which I took, and said that if I had any company to take them into the front room, and when the dinner bell rang to come to his table. In a few days Mr. Henry Goddard came out with a market basket his wife had filled with everything nice, for she thought I was eating the jail food. I thanked him and said that I was eating at Mr. Webster's table and would be pleased to see him any time, but he need not take the trouble to bring any food. I could not see why it was that Mr. Goddard and Mr. Webster took such an interest in an entire stranger. When the overseers visited the house for their monthly suppers, they visited my room and we had a social smoke, and they invited me to dine with them. Mr. Samuel Carleton was one of the overseers at that time. Many captains and merchants came out to visit me. When Mrs. Webster wanted a nice pigeon dinner, I found an old flint-lock gun, cleaned it up, and put a row of corn out in the back yard. The pigeons came after the corn in great numbers, and I fired and picked up sixteen dead ones. A few days later seven or eight prisoners broke out of the House of Correction and all escaped to the woods. The police and constables were hunting day and night and succeeded in capturing some. Mr. William Huse called at the house and wanted me to go into the country with him. I told him that I was a prisoner and could not leave. He said that he had seen Mr. Webster and that I could go if I wished. Mr. Webster readily consented, saying that he was not afraid of my running away. So we started out, going as far as Baldwin the first night, which we spent at a tavern there. The next day we met a farmer, who had given two fellows their breakfast that morning, whose description tallied with that of two confidence men from Boston who were among the escaped fugitives. We traced the fugitives to North Berwick, and found that they had taken the westward train. Mr. Huse telegraphed to the Boston police, but they failed to secure the men.

After my return to the work-house Mr. Webster told me I might send for my wife. I did so, and she was with me some three weeks. While there Mr. Cheney, the turnkey, lost his wife and had to be away a few days. So Mr. Webster got me to take his place. At that time there were thirty-two prisoners in the house. On the Fourth of July, there being a great celebration in Portland and a great deal going on up on Munjoy Hill, Mr. Webster invited me to ride into the city with him. I told him that I did not think it would do for me to come in as I might meet some of the prosecuting officers. He said that it would be all right as long as he was with me. While driving up Congress Street on to Munjoy Hill we met Mr. George F. Shepley coming down. He looked at me very sharply, and I said to Mr. Webster that he would hear from Shepley. The next day he did receive a letter from him with orders to keep Willard close as he was seen in the city the day before. When my time expired I paid the $20 fine and left for home.

I wish to say to Mr. Cox, ship keeper, that when he is about to leave this world, to make a full statement of the facts from the time he went on board the ship "Antelope" until he left, and to publish that statement in the daily papers so that my friends may see it, as I may not be here at that time.

Capt. David Jones was intimately acquainted with Capt. John Smith, and corresponded with him after his arrival at Liverpool. In a letter from Captain Smith he said that the pilot took the ship to sea ignorant of the true facts, and that he (Smith) took that course to get his ship clear. Mr. Jones had the contents of that letter printed in the daily papers. Had I known the true facts of the case, I could have very easily left the ship after giving the captain his course, and let him wake the keeper and set him ashore with the ship's boat at Portland Head.

CHAPTER VI.

IN WHICH A SWORD FISH IS HARPOONED. — IT PROVES A NOVELTY IN PORTLAND. — HOW I PILOTED A DISABLED STEAMER INTO PORT. — THE PERILOUS EXPERIENCE OF A PILOT. — PULLING DROWNING MEN OUT OF THE WATER. — A FAMOUS CAMPING-OUT CLUB. — HEN HAWKS FOR DINNER. — THE FATHER OF THE FINNAN HADDIE INDUSTRY AND HIS SKILL AT QUOITS.

THE summer of 1858 I caught my first sword-fish in a lapped-streak, centreboard sail-boat, fourteen feet long. Capt. B. F. Willard, a cousin, was with me. We went to Rock Cod Ledge to catch mackerel, taking harpoon, lance, and line with us. While on the ledge, fishing, we saw a fin, supposed it to be a shark, made sail and started for it. When I got nearer I saw that it was no shark, but a sword-fish. He saw us, and started away. I threw the harpoon and hit him in a good place, giving him all the line and holding on to the end. The sail was rolled up and taken down, the fish towing the boat after him. After some time he got tired and we began to haul on him slowly, coiling the line into the tub carefully as we hauled. When we got him in sight of the boat he started away and we gave him line, clear to the end again. Then I saw his sword, and he was the most wicked looking fish that I ever put eyes on. In fact, I was much afraid he would come through the boat. We did not haul on him again for nearly an hour. As he lay motionless on the bottom we supposed he was dead, and hauled him up carefully. When alongside and the gaff in him, I took the lance and lanced him four or five times

SWORD-FISH.—LENGTH, 21 FEET; WEIGHT, 953 POUNDS; CAPTURED AUGUST 29, 1868.

to make sure he was dead. We had all that we could do to get him into the boat. On arriving home we took him into Mr. K. D. Atwood's fish market to exhibit. When he was measured he was seventeen feet in length. This was the first sword-fish I ever saw landed in Portland. He was on exhibition two days. The market was crowded most of the time to see the monster. The two days brought us in $167 in ten-cent pieces. Then he was skinned and mounted. At that time there were not ten pounds of that kind of meat sold, as people were not acquainted with it. I would, when musters were in the city, get a tent of Mr. Fowler, the sail-maker, and put it on exhibition, with a life-size painting of the fish on the outside of the tent. I would take from $40 to $50 a day. After keeping it two years, I sold the fish for $25.

How I Piloted the "North American" in.—In the winter of 1858–59 it was severely cold. I was then on the pilot boat "Alida." She set low in the water, her draft was six feet, and she was a good, safe boat, but very wet in a strong breeze. I had one particularly hard trip in her while looking for the steamship "North American," Captain McMaster, from Liverpool. After being out seven days and nights my man was taken sick, and I came to land him, shipping Capt. B. F. Willard in his place. While doing this, Captain Crawford, port captain of the Allan line, brought me a telegram that the steamship had touched at Halifax and was due here. In coming out she had run into Cape Race and stove a hole in her bow, the forward compartment filling. We at once turned the boat about and went outside, staying there as long as we could. The vapor became so thick that we could not see Portland Light, and the boat iced up badly; so we stood inside Ram Island Ledge, where the island made some shelter, and anchored. The wind was north northeast and blowing very heavy.

About midnight our anchor rope chafed off and it took us some little time to get our heavy clothing on. We got forward and hauled in the rope. By this time we were drifting out by the ledge, where the sea was running sharp. We hoisted the head of the jib, wore around and hoisted close-reefed mainsail, and steered in for Bangs Island. The vapor was so thick we could not see three boats' length. While steering in, the big anchor was got ready and one end of the line made fast round the foremast. When breakers were sighted near the Point we luffed to, anchored, and furled the sail. I did not dare to go inside the Point for fear of the heavy drift ice coming down the bay. The night being very cold, we took one-hour watches. The boat was dipping her bowsprit and making ice very fast, and the man on deck kept busy breaking it off. It was B. J. Willard on the starboard watch and B. F. Willard on the port, and the coffee kept hot all night. We had no sleep, but went below by turns long enough to get warm.

Before daylight the wind canted in and the water became smooth. At daybreak the boat was a sight to see; she had settled over two feet by the head, and her bowsprit, jib, foot ropes, bobstay, and bowsprit guys were one solid mass of ice. By nine o'clock the vapor had so settled that we could see the top of Portland Head Light. Soon after, my brother William, who was towing out a brig with the tow-boat "Tiger," steamed over to me and said there was no clear water inside Bangs Island. As my boat was unmanageable, I towed in with him.

On arrival in town I went to Captain Crawford and reported it impossible to stay out any longer in the pilot boat; that the only way was to watch from the Observatory day and night until the ship was sighted. As he agreed with me I took rockets and blue lights to the tug boat and hired a man to watch from the Observatory the first night, introducing him to Mr. Moody, who was always ready to render any kindness in his power. In the morning I went to relieve my watchman; and about ten o'clock, the vapor having settled, I sighted the ship's flag above the woods on Bangs Island. Then I ran for the tug boat, and the crew happening to be there we started off at once. After passing Ram Island Ledge we ran into thick vapor, and, though I knew about the direction to go, I could not tell whether the vessel was under way or anchored. Finally we heard a gun, but the report was confusing. When the port gun, toward us, was fired, it would sound close by; but the starboard gun sounded a long distance away, as though the ship were making off. However, we kept on running for the sound and blowing our whistle, and when within two miles of Cod Ledge found the ship at anchor in quite deep water. Captain McMaster said he never was so glad to see any man in his life as he was to see me, as he had begun to be deeply troubled over the danger he was in, and signs of a big snow-storm were multiplying. We steamed in slowly, on account of the pressure of water against the bulkhead. I took my station at the foretop to look over the vapor if possible. When within half a mile of Ram Island the tops of the trees on Bangs Island could be seen, as well as Portland Head Light. When I came down to the pilot bridge both my ears were frozen. It began to snow just as we reached the wharf.

After the cargo was discharged the ship went to Portsmouth Navy Yard dock for repairs, and I went with her. On the way there the water was two feet higher in the forward compartment than outside the ship. Old sails were stuck in the forepeak and shored up with spars to stop some of the pressure of water. When in the dry-dock she showed where she hit the bluff at Cape Race; it was the fourteen-feet mark on the cut-water, and from there round the forefoot. Fifteen feet of the keel had slewed off sideways, driving the cut-water into the ship some three feet. Her bowsprit struck the cliff at the same time.

SAVING A MAN FROM DROWNING.—One day, while walking along Commercial Street, I saw several men running for Burnham's Wharf, and hastened there to see what the trouble was. The wharf was covered with men looking down into the dock. I crowded through them, and looking down I saw a man drowning. I immediately pulled off my hat and coat and jumped in, feet first, behind him. It being low tide and about seven feet of water, I stuck in the mud, but kicked myself out and came up. When I got to the surface he was just sinking. I caught hold of his collar and swam with him up to the piling. He had just life enough left to hold on to the piling with both arms. I put one arm on the next pile and held him up with the other, and in a few minutes a boat came with two men from the next wharf. The man was well filled up with salt water and something stronger, I judged by the smell. I immediately went to work on him, holding his head down for a few seconds for the water to run out, and then holding it up for him to breathe. While I was doing this the men were rowing the boat around to Maine Wharf steps. When he got on the wharf he was able to walk with the assistance of his friends. This was the second man that I have saved from drowning by jumping overboard after them, and holding them up until a boat came to my assistance. In all cases you must keep behind drowning men, as they will grapple anything that they can get hold of, and if they once get hold of you it will be impossible for you to swim; in that case both will sink at once. I do not approve of rolling a person on a barrel to get the water out of him, as the water will rush into the throat and strangle him. The life saving station has the best method of treating such cases.

The "Nettle" and Her Fortunes. — In the fall of 1859 I sold my pilot boat, "Alida," went to Boston, and bought the schooner yacht "Nettle"; she being a much larger and safer one than the "Alida," and a good sailor. I fitted her up for a pilot boat and put "No. 1" in her mainsail. I used her for piloting in the winter and pleasure parties to the islands in the summer, as well as parties for deep-sea fishing. I had a large, safe dory built, that would seat twenty-three persons, to land at the islands. This boat came in use for catching big fish. In the warm weather I had all the business that I could attend to. Mr. Daniel Gould, my partner, meantime looked after the stevedoring, which was beginning to increase. I have seen, from sunrise to sunset, sixteen cargoes of molasses arrive in the harbor from Cuba. At that time they began to lay the railroad tracks down on the wharves and fill them with lumber and shook so we could not work on wheels. Some time later, by advice of Mr. John B. Curtis, I built a scow and put a hoisting engine in it and all the equipments to discharge a vessel. That proved a big success, because it could go anywhere a vessel did. As business increased, the steam hoisters increased. At the present time nearly all the hoisting is done by steam; an average day's work by steam and one gang being 300 tons of coal per day.

In the summer of 1860 arrivals of coal and salt were on the fast increase, and the wharves were well filled up with square-rigged vessels, bringing cargoes and taking them away. It was nothing unusual to see, at that time, several barks and brigs beating out or in the harbor as the case might be. That summer the mackerel fishermen were getting good fares, and there was still good mackerel fishing in Casco Bay. Late in the season of 1860 I took several mackerel parties out to Rock Cod Ledge, where they had abundant success.

A FAMOUS CAMPING-OUT CLUB.—In the summer of 1861 I took the Giojelliere Club to Jewell's Island (giojelliere is Italian for jeweler) to camp out for two weeks, a trip that was repeated for four seasons. The following were the club members: G. A. Thomas, John L. Shaw, George M. Howe, Thomas McEwan, Alex D. Reeves, Charles H. Sawyer, John K. Paine, Sewall W. Thrasher, Charles Carlton, William H. Dennett, William W. Colby, Jarvis Stevens, Waldstein Phillips, Sumner C. Fernald. The pilot boat "Nettle" was kept in attendance while they were in camp. In pleasant weather the boat was used after breakfast for deep-sea fishing. Plenty of cod and mackerel were caught for their own use. One trip on Rock Cod Ledge we sighted a large sword-fish, harpooned him, and in about half an hour had him on board. I consider Jewell's Island the best place for camping out there is in Casco Bay; plenty of fine clams near the camping-ground, and lots of nice eggs, milk, and butter from a farm near at hand.

THE "NETTLE" IN A HIGH WIND, GOING TO SQUARE-RIG VESSEL OFF SHORE.

Captain Chase, the owner of the island, was very kind to us, and took particular pride in pointing out the places where it was reported people had dug up great treasures buried by Captain Kidd, the famous pirate; but all the digging we did was for clams—they were rich enough for us. The club had a highly original code of rules; one of them forbidding all sleep the last night of the stay, and another commanding the kindling of a big bonfire on that occasion. Captain Chase gave us all the trees we wanted for the purpose. One day each season was set apart for shooting on the other islands; sandpeeps and plovers being in especial demand. All the game, whatever it might be, had to be cooked. I brought in a hen hawk one time. The bird looked nice and brown when brought to the table. Being the man who shot it I had to do the carving, but my invitation to partake met with dead silence. Nobody seemed to be hankering for hen hawk. It looked so dainty that I was tempted, and cut a piece out of the breast. When I put my teeth into the slice a most horrible oil seemed to come up round them. I did not get the bad taste out of my mouth for a month. The last night was always given up to frolic; and blacking the faces of the drowsy folks, putting raw clams in their boots, and similar sinful games were indulged in by the more mischievous ones.

There was a great deal of quoit pitching during the camping out; four pounders being thrown sixty-three feet by the experts. Mr. Thomas McEwan (the first man to smoke finnan haddies in Portland and the originator of that flourishing industry here) was the champion player and I was his partner. Many times he was challenged by his Scotch friends to contests of skill with the quoits, and he invariably won.

CHAPTER VII.

PORTLAND HARBOR IN WAR TIME.— MUCH TANGLED RED TAPE.— RUSHING ASSOCIATED PRESS NEWS TO THE SHORE.— PERILOUS EXPERIENCE OF A COAST PILOT.— THE CLOSE SHAVE OF THE "ANGLO SAXON."— SUDDEN DEATH OF MY FATHER.

IN the fall of 1861, it being war time and particular caution needed, Mr. J. L. Farmer and myself went to Fort Preble to see the captain in charge of the fort in order to fix signals so the mail steamships could pass on up to the city. They were fixed at five whistles of five seconds each. The fort was to give the ship one blue light; the ship to respond with one whistle and pass on. If no blue light was given, the order was to anchor the ship and go on shore to report. This went on well for a time. The whistle was to be given when abreast of the wharf at Bangs Island.

One bitter cold night I was taking in one of the mail ships and got no answer to the whistle; so anchored the ship, lowered the boat, and went to the fort. The wind was very strong and cold. We hailed the sentinel. After waiting some ten minutes, an officer and a few men came down to the boat, asking all manner of questions. The officer wanted to know why I did not give proper signals. I told him I gave the signals arranged before going to the ship, and waited for the fort signal to pass; but no signal was given. He then gave me orders to pass. The next day I called on the captain at Fort Preble and stated my case. The fact was the sentinel was asleep, and he was punished for it. Then the signals were changed.

The same whistles were given, and if I got no answer I was to pass on. If I got a blue light I was to anchor the ship and report to the fort. That, too, worked well for a time, as they could sleep and the ship pass up to the wharf. A little later I was taking a mail ship in, got by the fort, and was nearly in range of Fort Gorges, when Fort Preble sent a cannon ball across our bow and very near us. As we heard it scream, going through the air, the captain of the ship asked if they were going to shoot us. I told him that I gave the proper signal. The ship was then anchored. The officer heard the chain running out, luckily for us, as he might have kept on firing. The boat was lowered, and, lantern in hand, we landed. I walked up the wharf and passing the wood pile saw the flash of a musket. I began to think my last hour had come. I understood some time afterwards that the gun was fired to bring the guard. The sentinel cried, "Halt." I did so and waited some time in the cold. Finally an officer and ten men came in sight with a lantern. When within ten feet of me he halted his men, and asked, "Who comes there," or something like it. I said, "Willard, the pilot." Then he asked me why I did not give the signal. I told him I gave the signal as arranged by his captain. After a lot more questions he let us pass, though at one time he thought of putting a squad of men on board. The next day I called on the fort captain and a new code of signals was arranged, which worked very well until transports came for government stores to take South. Then there was no end of trouble. The first transport I boarded had but one rusty old gun that we were obliged to "squib out" to see if it would work; and several that followed had no guns at all. So we went back to whistles, and these had to be changed often for fear the Confederates would learn the code. One of the ships that came for government supplies was the well-known "Great Republic." When mailships came into the harbor, night or day (this was before the Atlantic cable began to work), I took the associated dispatches, fastened them to a line and lowered it from the bridge to a boat provided by Mr. Ira Berry for the purpose; his design being to save all the time possible in getting the news on the wires to New York. He could not wait for the ship to dock.

THE BITTER EXPERIENCE OF A PILOT.—The life of a pilot is but a hard one at its best, and his perils are many. One day I took the steamship "Indian," Captain Jones, out, and the weather being calm concluded not to bother the tug, but return alone in my little boat. But by the time we were passing Portland Head a high sea and wind rose and it became very rough. When the ship was a safe distance outside she hove to so that I might leave. The boat was lowered and I watched my chance to drop into her. It came and I sheered off from the ship's side, singing out to her people to let go of my bow painter; but happening to look over my shoulder I saw the bow line becoming taut. Coming on top of a sea at the same time the boat rolled over bottom up, with me under it and the water gurgling in my ears. The next sea turned her right side up and I called to haul up, watching my chance to seize the ship ladder. In this I succeeded, and my boat was hauled up by the bow line. Captain Jones wanted me to go across to Liverpool with him, insisting that my boat could never live in that sea. But I told him to stop the ship and head for the Two Lights. At this time we were abreast Bell Rock. He ordered a life-preserver put in the boat, and pressed a stiff horn of brandy on me, but the latter I declined, telling him that if I was going to be drowned I wanted to die sober.

This time, though with difficulty, I cleared the ship's side safely, and started for home. The sea was running very high as the passengers crowded to the rail to watch my course, and the captain sent some men into the rigging for a lookout. I did not have to row much as the wind and high sea drove me on even faster than I wished to go. When high combers came I had to back water with both oars, to steady the boat from running too fast and from broaching. This had to be done until Bangs Island Point was reached. There I got smooth water and pulled hard for Simonton's Cove. It was nearly dark when I reached there, thoroughly chilled, and went to my father's house to get warm and pass the night.

I think that Captain Jones was as fine a captain as ever walked a ship's deck. He was a great favorite among his passengers, and always had good luck on quick passages. Later, when he was in the steamship "Hungarian," from Liverpool to Portland, I was out looking for his ship some three or four days, and expecting to see her come in sight every moment. At the end of the fourth day I saw the steam tug "Uncle Sam," with my brother William, coming to bring me the news that the ship "Hungarian," with all hands, was lost on Cape Sable.

THE CLOSE SHAVE OF THE "ANGLO SAXON."—One time I was out looking for the steamship "Anglo Saxon," and had my brother Henry and Capt. Granville Lowell with me. We were out about seven days and nights. The ship was making a long passage. I felt sure that she would heave in sight the seventh night, as she had favorable weather for the last two or three days. It was a dark night and stormy, and the wind north northeast, but the lights could be seen plainly. About midnight a light was sighted outside. As it came nearer we thought it must be the steamship as the light was brighter than on sailing vessels. Thinking it strange she sent up no rockets or blue lights, we burnt a blue light; but got no answer. As she got nearer we could see that it was the "Anglo Saxon" without doubt. We tacked ship and went to burning blue lights and then a torch; the torch being made of oakum saturated with kerosene and tied to a boat hook.

The ship was running away from us fast. Though we had rockets aboard, the spray was coming over the pilot boat so fast we could not use them. After a while we attracted attention and the ship stopped. At that time all ships ran for Portland Head Light, bearing northwest by north, but the "Anglo Saxon" was drifting fast for Trundy's Reef Shoal, as I found by taking the bearing of the light when near her stern. I leaped on board, fearing every moment that she would strike bottom, and sang out at the top of my voice, "Hard to port and full speed ahead." Then I ran to the pilot bridge, telling the captain that the vessel might strike any instant, as she was so near the ledge I could not tell where the buoy was. I still anxiously watched the compass, and in a few minutes she changed her bearing for Portland Head and I felt safe. Then I drew a long breath, as I let the captain know it was the closest shave I ever saw a ship in and get out safe.

When asked why he did not send up rockets while approaching, the captain replied that it was so rough he didn't think the pilot boat would be out such a night. He supposed the blue light was a ship signaling for a pilot, and thought he was heading off. I told him I did not wonder he thought so, for he passed me like a greyhound. Seeing the lights in the saloon convinced me that it was the "Anglo Saxon," no other ship being due at that time. She was getting short of coal, had steamed slowly for one or two days, and was using up all the spare spars, fenders, and steerage berths. We finally got the ship to the city and docked her safely. She had just a wheelbarrow full of coal left on reaching port.

I stayed on the wharf the rest of the night looking for the pilot boat and feeling a good deal worried. As she could only fetch Pond Cove or the Black Rocks on the first tack I feared she would have a perilous time. A little after daybreak I saw her coming round Spring Point. It seems that she came near running into Trundy's Reef buoy, the main boom just swinging over it. She was five hours beating from the Black Rocks by Portland Head. When heading off she would dive into the sea up to the foremast, and it was impossible to make much headway in such high seas; but the boat did not fail to tack every time they wanted it to. Captain Lowell suggested to my brother Henry to run out round the cape and go to Wood Island, but Henry refused, saying that if worst came to worst he would run her ashore in Alewive Cove.

MY FATHER'S SUDDEN DEATH. — My father was a fisherman all his life, and went upon the water nearly every suitable day. He was noted for his unusual good judgment about running in thick weather. On the morning of June 3, 1863, he went from Simonton's Cove to Richmond Island, in a Hampton boat, with a small boy as companion, to get bait. The two stayed at the island all night, and next morning went to the fishing grounds, where they set their trawls and anchored their boat for hand-line fishing. After fishing for a time the boy hooked a halibut. Father went forward to handle the fish, the boy put the gaff in, and between the two they hauled it into the boat. There it began to struggle, and as my father bent over to finish it he fell back into the boat dead.

The boy shouted to Mr. John Stillwell, who was fishing in a boat quite a distance from them. Mr. Stillwell, seeing only one man in the boat where a moment before he had seen two, thought something was wrong and hastened to lend assistance. As the boy felt confident of his ability to bring the boat in unaided after the mast was set, and haul the trawl too, Mr. Stillwell took father in his own boat and brought him to the cove. When he arrived at the beach I happened to be there. The doctor, who was hastily summoned, pronounced the cause of death to be the bursting of a blood vessel on the brain.

The boy, who is now Mr. Edward Field, Superintendent of Government Fortifications at Portland Head, brought his boat in safely, and received many a compliment, as well as something more substantial, for his presence of mind and the skill he displayed.

CHAPTER VIII.

CAPTURE OF THE "CALEB CUSHING" AND THE "ARCHER" BY CONFEDERATE PRIVATEERS. — THE BOLD ATTEMPT IN PORTLAND HARBOR. — A DAY OF EXCITEMENT IN THE CITY. — SOLDIERS AND CITIZENS TO THE RESCUE. — BLOWING UP OF THE "CUSHING" AND RECAPTURE OF THE "ARCHER." — CONFEDERATE PRISONERS IN FORT PREBLE. — HOW DANIEL GOULD CAME TO HIS DEATH.

ON the morning of the 27th of June, 1863, the city was thrown into great commotion by the news that the revenue cutter "Caleb Cushing" had been taken out of the harbor the night before by Lieutenant Reed, of the Confederate Navy, and his crew of twenty-one, and that she had been sighted off Green Island by the Observatory people.

The story of the daring seizure and subsequent recapture is familiar to those acquainted with the history of the Civil War, but may be new to some of my readers. Lieut. C. W. Reed, a commissioned officer of the Confederate Navy, was commander of the privateer "Tacony," which had committed many depredations on the northern coast and high seas, and was laden with considerable spoil. Learning that Federal cruisers were after him, and fearing recognition as his vessel had become pretty well known, Lieutenant Reed, after capturing the schooner "Archer," of Southport, on the 24th of June, transferred everything to her and burned the "Tacony." The "Archer" was then headed for Portland, for the purpose of cutting out the "Cushing," then lying in the stream, and destroying the uncompleted United States gunboats "Pontoone" and

CAPTURE AND BLOWING UP OF THE UNITED STATES REVENUE CUTTER "CALEB CUSHING," BY THE REBELS. OFF PORTLAND HARBOR. JUNE 27, 1863.

"Agawam," moored at Franklin Wharf, as well as other shipping that might be found in the harbor.

While on the way two Falmouth fishermen, Albert P. Bibber and Elbridge Titcomb, who were hauling their trawl in a small boat about eight miles to the southeast of Damariscove Island, were captured by Reed, whose intention was to use them as pilots; but they refused to so serve and were put in confinement. About sunset the "Archer" came to harbor to the eastward of Pomeroy's Rock, off Fish Point. At this place the privateer remained, waiting for the opportunity to carry the audacious design into execution. The clearness of the night, it is believed, deterred them from accomplishing the whole of their daring purpose.

THE DARING ATTEMPT IN PORTLAND HARBOR. —About two o'clock in the morning a detachment from the "Archer" approached the "Cushing" with muffled oars, and boarded her, gagging and ironing the watch. Lieutenant Davenport, the officer in charge, was seized as soon as he came on deck, and the crew, about twenty in number, placed in irons. The cutter was then towed out of the harbor by the way of Hussey's Sound, thus avoiding the forts, followed by the "Archer." Reed passed through the passage between Cow Island and Hog Island, standing out to sea by Green Island. At ten o'clock in the morning he was about fifteen miles from the city, when the wind died away and left him becalmed.

PORTLAND TO THE RESCUE.—On hearing of the audacious attempt all Portland was in arms, and energetic measures were taken by Mayor McClellan and Customs Collector Jewett. Steamers in the harbor were pressed into service and volunteers enrolled. I learned that the Boston steamer "Forest City," Capt.

CAPT. JOHN LISCOMB, STEAMER "FOREST CITY." JUNE 27, 1863.

John Liscomb, was getting ready to go to the rescue, and so went down to the boat. Captain Liscomb said he was getting up steam and going over to Fort Preble to get men and guns. It being low tide the steamer could not get up to the wharf, and I suggested that I had a large boat and would take whatever was wanted to the steamer. He readily closed with the offer and told me to take the boat along.

On arriving near the fort, a large number of men from the regulars were boated off with rifles, and spare muskets furnished to the volunteers. Two brass field pieces were also taken on board. Then we started for the captured cutter. On passing Bangs Island Point, I went to the foremast head with opera glasses and could make her out in the haze a long distance off. There was a light wind to the eastward and she was headed to the south. We at once cleared for action.

When within a mile and a half of the cutter we were in her wake, running straight for her. Then she tacked, and we could see her men getting the midship pivot gun ready. Captain Liscomb ported his helm and stood to the west. Presently the gun was discharged, and the shot, a thirty-two pounder, came skipping over the water, falling just short of the steamer. It was a good line shot. At this time the New York boat "Chesapeake," which had also been pressed into service, and was swarming with armed men, came up. Just then the wind died away to a calm, and it became evident that the cutter could not be handled by her captors. It was decided to board her, and I manned the big boat with rifles and put off.

When within a hundred yards of the cutter, we saw three boats put off, and, at the same time, flames coming out of her companion way. We at once held back, fearing that the magazine would explode. My men were very anxious to use their rifles on the escaping privateers. Capt. George Willard was in the bow, and I saw him leveling his gun at them, saying that he "wanted one." I ordered him to stop, pointing to a white hankerchief on a boat hook, sticking up in the bow of the nearest boat, and telling him that it was a flag of truce, or signal of surrender, which must not be fired upon; but it was with the utmost difficulty that I could restrain my men. While the men were tumbling over the ship's side, I saw Capt. Albert Bibber among them. The "Forest City" picked him up, and he told them where the "Archer" was. The steamer at once started for the "Archer" and soon captured her, finding Bob Mullins, a New Orleans Confederate, in charge.

BLOWING UP THE "CALEB CUSHING."—Meanwhile the cutter blew up, sinking stern first in thirty-three fathoms of water. After sinking, the spars came up with the burnt rigging attached. The wreck was soon surrounded by the steamers "Forest City" and "Chesapeake," the tugs "Uncle Sam" and "Tiger," and the fishing schooner "E. A. Williams." All the men in the boats were captured and landed at Fort Preble, from whence they were transferred to Fort Warren in Boston Harbor, and exchanged some sixteen months later. We learned from them that they only found one thirty-two pound shot in the locker, and were obliged to load afterwards with spikes and old iron kettles, which they broke up. As we were right astern of them, they failed by one or two points to train the gun on us. The shot that came nearest to us fell short about twenty yards.

When I got to Custom House Wharf, I met Lieutenant Davenport, of the cutter, who wanted a gang of men to discharge the "Archer," as what goods she had were going to the Custom House for storage; so I put a gang on the vessel. My partner, Daniel Gould, also had men on the wharf loading truck teams, and was directing their movements. My gang found about twenty-five loaded muskets in the salt room; and, on asking the lieutenant what disposition to make of them, we were told to put them on the port side, muzzle to the brake of the quarter-deck. In discharging the "Archer," we found chests, trunks, valises, clothes-bags, chronometers, and spy-glasses, part of the plunder of ships captured by the privateers. There was a great deal of excitement in the city, many threats were made against the prisoners, and the wharves were crowded with throngs of curious people. Lieutenant Davenport placed a guard alongside the vessel to keep strangers from going on board; but, still, some slipped by.

THE LAMENTABLE DEATH OF DANIEL GOULD.—While my men were busy passing things out to the wharf, a longshoreman, named John Sidney, slipped aboard unnoticed by the guard. Wandering about to gratify his curiosity, he picked up a musket and carelessly cocked it; thinking, as so many foolish men before and since have thought under similar circumstances, that it was unloaded. It was high water at the time and the vessel was level with the wharf. He pulled the trigger and discharged the musket, the ball entering Mr. Daniel Gould's thigh, passing through both legs and seriously wounding a man near by. Mr. Gould was at once taken home and amputation decided necessary by the doctors. He died under the knife—the only man who lost his life during the whole affair of the "Cushing." Sidney was arrested and put in jail. I was called upon by the city marshal to give my opinion of the shooting, and told him that I knew Sidney well; that the man had worked for both Mr. Gould and myself; that he was of kindly disposition, and that I was convinced that the discharge of the musket was purely accidental. So the man was discharged. Shortly after this I started a subscription paper for Mr. Gould's family. I collected $850; $200 of this amount came from Boston through Custom-House Collector Jewett. I was sent for to come to the Custom House, as he said there were $200 he wished me to receipt for. I asked him whom we should thank for it, and he said that the parties did not wish to be known. A small house and lot of land were bought at Simonton's Cove, of Mr. John Woodbury, and deeded to Mr. Gould's family. Mr. Gould's last words to me were to look out for his family. I told him that I would, and I have done so faithfully.

The capture and recapture of the "Cushing" were among the most notable incidents of the Civil War; and peculiarly interesting to Portland people because, for the first time, those at home were brought face to face with armed Confederates. Nor was it less interesting to the South, where the daring though unsuccessful attempt to enter a New England port and surprise its shipping was regarded as an heroic exploit. We looked upon it as a piratical undertaking. The Southern side of the story, though in all essential facts the same that I have told, has an interest of its own as coming from the defeated party in the struggle. It was related for the first time by Robert Hunt, one of the crew of the "Tacony," in a paper read in the fall of 1894 before the Confederates' Veteran Association of Savannah, and republished in the *Portland Press* of October 27th in the same year.

CHAPTER IX.

THE CONFEDERATE ACCOUNT OF THE CAPTURE OF THE "CALEB CUSHING."— MR. HUNT'S VIVACIOUS STORY.— HOW THE PRIVATEERS STOLE INTO THE HARBOR, STOLE OUT, AND WERE CAUGHT WITH THE GOODS IN THEIR POSSESSION.— THE FISH CHOWDER ON BOARD THE "ARCHER," AND THE HUMBLE PIE THE PRIVATEERS AFTERWARDS ATE.

THE Confederate side of the story of the capture and recapture of the "Caleb Cushing," mentioned in the preceding chapter and told by Mr. Robert Hunt, is a vivacious narrative, well worth repeating in this connection. "One night in June," says Mr. Hunt, "the Confederate cruiser 'Tacony' lay becalmed forty-five miles from Portland Harbor. We had been," he adds, "for several days burning and bonding Yankee merchantmen, and now among the fishermen, several of whom we had captured and destroyed. About six bells of the first watch, as well as I can remember, our lookout reported a steamer ahead; our commander came on deck and after scanning the steamer with his glasses pronounced her a Yankee gunboat. 'Well, boys,' he said, 'I guess our frolics are over, but we must try and fool them.' She was soon in hailing distance and as she hauled up her commander hailed us as follows: 'Bark ahoy, what and where bound?' to which Lieutenant Reed answered: 'Bark "Mary Jane" from Sagua La Grande, bound to Portland.' The captain of the gunboat then informed us that there was a Rebel privateer cruising along the coast and burning merchantmen and that we had better keep a sharp lookout.

Lieutenant Reed thanked him and he steamed away to the southward. What a narrow escape; we were all speechless; for more than a minute not a word was passed. The silence was broken by Reed, whose first words were: 'Boys, we have had a close call, but we are still on deck. It is getting too hot for us in this latitude, we must change the programme.' It was pretty generally known in the northern and eastern ports that we were cruising off the coast, and several gunboats and cutters had been sent out in search of us. Lieutenant Reed ordered all hands aft and stated to us his plans, which were as follows: To capture a smart schooner, burn the 'Tacony,' go into Portland, burn the two gunboats, then about completed, capture one of the Boston steamers, burn the revenue cutter, put to sea, make for southern waters, and join the 'Florida.'

"The next afternoon we captured a smart looking little fishing schooner called the 'Archer.' Her crew were just about sitting down to a nice fish supper. Their captain asked us to join them, and as they had a first-class chowder, besides some nice sounds and tongues cooked as they knew how to cook them, we accepted the invitation. After dark we transferred one six pounder, and such other articles as we needed, from the 'Tacony' to the 'Archer.' We then set fire to the 'Tacony' and stayed by her until she burned to the water's edge and sank. The next afternoon we anchored off Fish Point in Portland Harbor. All hands were below with the exception of a few knocking about the deck.

"Those below were employed making oakum balls and saturating them with turpentine, with which to set fire to the gunboats. At the last moment, when everything was in readiness and every man had received his instructions, our engineer, Mr. Brown, informed Lieutenant Reed that he didn't feel competent to take charge of the Boston steamer's engine. Lieutenant Reed then decided to capture the United States revenue cutter 'Caleb Cushing' and put to sea again. Two boats were manned, and were soon along-side of her and hailed by the lookout, but before he had time to hail again we were aboard and had him silenced. In a few moments we had the entire crew, thirty-five men, in irons."

The privateers made their way out of the harbor to Green Island, as has been related. There they were becalmed. From this point Mr. Hunt continues his story, as follows: "We found plenty of powder in the magazine, but no shot or shell. The cutter had received orders the day before to get ready for a cruise in search of the 'Tacony.' She had taken aboard her powder, and waited for the next day to take in her shot and shell; so we were informed by the crew. Our gunner found one thirty-two-pound shot in the potato locker, which he carried on deck. Our little breeze died away, and Reed ordered all hands below to get what rest they could. While I was looking astern, I saw what looked to be a steamer coming out, and, as I thought, heading for us. I called Reed, who came on deck, and, after looking at her awhile, said he guessed it was the Boston steamer bound out. He went below again, telling me to keep my eye on her. I shortly discovered another steamer astern of her, also coming out, and, on looking through the glasses at the first steamer, saw a crowd of soldiers on the upper deck. I immediately called our commander, and, on his reaching the deck and after one glance at the steamers, he called all hands to clear the deck for action. The thirty-two pounder was loaded (it was located amidships), and the order given to put the helm down, the gunner and crew in the meantime training the gun to get a range on the steamer. The cutter would not mind her helm. 'Hard down.' shouted Reed, jumping toward the helm. 'Hard down, it is,' I answered. 'O, for a six-knot breeze and a few shot or shell,' cried Reed; 'we would show them some fun!'

"The steamers were directly in our wake, and when Reed saw that we could not get an effective shot at them, he said: 'We will give them a scare anyhow!' The gun was trained as far aft as possible, and the order given to fire. When the smoke cleared away, both steamers were broadside to as if turning back, and we gave a yell and shouted, 'Load her up again,' but we had nothing to load her with. We had plenty of powder, but nary a shot or shell. Reed at once gave orders to set fire to the cutter and abandon her. The prisoners were brought on deck, put in two boats, given the key to their irons, and turned adrift. I jumped down into the cabin and proceeded to break up the furniture and collect the bedding to set on fire. When the order was given to set fire, I struck a match and in an instant the whole cabin was on fire. I rushed for the companion way, and when I reached the deck I was pretty badly scorched, eyebrows, lashes, and mustache singed, and face and hands pretty well blistered. At this time all hands were in the boats, with the exception of the gunner and myself. He had gathered up a lot of scrap iron, nails, spikes, etc., with which he had loaded the gun for a parting shot.

"Although the steamers were dead astern and not

within three or four points of the range of the gun, they both stopped when the last shot was fired. We pulled away from the cutter and lay on our oars, knowing that it would be useless to try to get away. Reed ordered us to throw our arms overboard, and every man stood up in the boats, unbuckled their belts, to which were attached our revolvers and cutlasses, and dropped them over the sides, and, I suppose, they are still lying at the bottom of Portland Bay. Reed then produced a shot bag of specie, which he divided among us. Our next act was to tie a white handkerchief to our boot hook and await our fate. The first steamer had been steering directly for us from the time that we abandoned the cutter. The other stopped to pick up the crew of the cutter. We noticed that when the first steamer got near us, a detachment of soldiers on the upper deck had their muskets aimed directly at us as if about to fire, but an officer sprang in front of them, with a drawn sword, and they at once came to a shoulder. We were ordered along-side, a rope was thrown to us, and we were taken on board. One man at a time was allowed to come over the side. He was searched, and then his arms tied behind his back with a piece of rattling stuff, and placed under guard before another was taken on board. There were not less than three hundred soldiers and armed citizens aboard the boat."

CHAPTER X.

THE WRECK OF THE "BOHEMIAN."— SCENES AND INCIDENTS OF THAT MEMORABLE DISASTER. — HOW THE ILL-FATED STEAMER WENT ASHORE. — A NOTABLE CAMPAIGN ORATOR AMONG THE SURVIVORS.—FISHING UP CASES OF GOODS.— MR. FARMER, CAPTAIN SARGENT, AND THE COOK STOVE. — THE DIVER WHO TOOK A NAP AT THE BOTTOM OF THE SEA.

ON the morning of February 23, 1864, the people of Portland were startled by the news of the wreck of the steamer "Bohemian," lost on the Cape Elizabeth shore early the night before. The "Bohemian," Captain Bolan, was one of the Montreal Ocean Line, running between Liverpool and Portland — a Clyde built, iron-screw steamer, about five years old. She was not accounted a fast vessel, but had often been tested by adverse winds and rough weather and found staunch. She left Liverpool on the 4th of February with two hundred and eighteen passengers and a crew consisting of ninety-nine men. Her passage was tedious and she was some days overdue. On the night of February 22d she was running slowly, and feeling her way into the harbor, when, about eight o'clock, she struck on Alden's Rock, just as the watch was being changed. She was headed for the shore, but began to sink, and the boats, six in number (each capable of holding sixty-five persons), were launched. All reached the shore in safety except boat No. 2, which was swamped while being launched. By this mishap forty-two lives were lost. Among the passengers who escaped was an Irish lad on his way to make his fortune in the New World.

He is now widely known as the Hon. John E. Fitzgerald, of Boston, a politician and popular campaign orator. Though his first reception on these shores was of the roughest, America has since made amends by the brilliant career she has offered to him. I was out in my pilot boat, "Nettle," looking for the ship for about five days, having with me Mr. Henry P. Miller, of Simonton's Cove. The day of the wreck I was off about ten miles from Portland Head. There was a light east wind and it was raining. I spoke two brigs, but they did not wish to take a pilot. We could then see three or four miles distant. I stayed in that locality until late in the afternoon. As the fog began to shut in I ran in for Portland Light. About six in the afternoon the wind died away, it became calm, and I anchored a mile southeast of Portland Head to hold my position. Thick fog hung over us and quite a swell was rolling in from the east. Mr. Miller had the first watch, from 8 to 12 P.M. Between eight and nine o'clock he called me and said that he heard a gun. I went on deck and asked him in what direction. He pointed, and I looked at the compass and said to him that it was in range of the Cape. I thought it could not be the ship in that direction. Asking him if the gun sounded loud, he said that it was too loud for a musket; and I told him if it was the ship we would hear another gun in a few minutes. We listened a long time, but heard no other, and made up our minds that they were celebrating on board some vessel, as it was Washington's birthday.

How We Heard of the Wreck.—At midnight it was my watch on deck. About two in the morning I heard a steamer coming out of the harbor, blowing her whistle. I blew the fog horn, so that the steamer would not run me down. As she came nearer, I blew oftener. When near they hailed me and wanted to know if it was the pilot boat. I recognized my brother's voice, and knew it was the steam tug "Uncle Sam." When near me my brother said that the steamship "Bohemian" was ashore on Broad Cove Rocks, and he wished me to go out with him. Some of the passengers were lost, he said. I took my boat, fog horn, and sounding-line and went aboard the tug, leaving Mr. Miller on board the pilot boat with orders to come out when the fog cleared and the wind breezed up. When on board the tug, I found the lieutenant of the cutter with his crew and boat in tow. After steaming a while I told him that he was running broad off and if he would stop I would take the boat and row to Broad Cove Rock. The lieutenant said that he would like to follow me; so I told him to take a sounding-line, as it would not do to get inside of six fathoms of water. After rowing for eight or ten minutes we were alongside Trundy's Reef buoy. The lieutenant thought that was straight going without having any compass in the boat. I told him that we must row outside of Broad Cove Rock and back in and sound as we went. We could hear the breakers on the rocks as we were backing in. We got as near to the breakers as we dared; and at that time I heard an iron door slam to the southwest, and said to the lieutenant that the "Bohemian" was not on the rock, but on the mainland. Every time my brother blew his whistle on the tug I blew the horn, so he could keep on the outside of me.

OUR FIRST SIGHT OF THE "BOHEMIAN."—When we got to the ship it was the hardest sight that I had ever looked at. We found Captain Bolan's boat and crew. He seemed to be completely prostrated over the loss of his ship and the passengers. When we got to the ship all of the passengers not lost were on shore. I learned that day from the chief officer that they were running in a west course, and intended running a half-hour longer. Then they were going to sound and then fire a gun. At that moment they saw faintly through the fog the two light-houses and knew it was the Cape by the revolving light. When made they were off the starboard beam. If they had not seen the lights in the course they were going, in ten or fifteen minutes the ship would have run on Richmond Island, or Watts Ledge, at full speed. It was said that the Boston boat sighted the "Bohemian" at the south of the Two Lights on her trip out. The chief officer said that after they had turned around they steered northeast to run down by the Cape. After running a while the ship struck on the bottom twice very heavily. It was soon found that she was making water. The helm was at once ordered to starboard. Evidently the ship was turning short of Broad Cove Rock. After the engine was stopped by the water coming up, the ship was anchored and orders given to fire the starboard gun. Before the port gun could be reached it was under water. That is the reason we only heard one gun in the pilot boat. The ship sank in six fathoms of water. If she had gone two ships' length ahead she would have sunk in ten fathoms, where most every one would have been lost.

THE "BOHEMIAN" GOES TO PIECES.—Mr. J. S. Miller was a passenger on the ship. He was the first to arrive in the city and give the sad news. Captain Barclay was put in charge of the ship, and divers were employed. A wrecking company, engaged to raise her, said they could box up the hatches, pump her out, and take her and her cargo to the city. Mr. Alvin Neal, myself, and others fished up a large number of passengers, and bags of mail near the starboard main gangway that were washed overboard from the steerage deck when the ship sank. Mr. J. L. Farmer thought as the ship was heading southeast and the topmast sent down she would lay easy so she could be pumped out in a few days. I told him that the first storm that came would break her up in a few hours. The ship lay there eleven days in perfectly smooth water, something never known before or since during the winter months. The wreckers kept at work boxing up the hatches. When about ready to use the pumps, there came an easterly gale. The ship went to pieces in a short time, and her cargo was scattered all over the Cape shore. The lighters could have taken all the bale goods out of the ship during that smooth weather, before the gale came. The morning after the gale the wind veered to the north. I got two extra men, put a tackle to the mast-head, and sailed out by the Cape, thinking that the current would take some of the cargo out that way. After passing the Cape I found the tide streak running about south southwest. When about eight miles from the Cape I began to get in wreckage, and some large cases of dry goods washing level with the water. The first case I got to I put on box hooks. When hoisted nearly out of the water the goods in it were so heavy the bottom came out, and I lost all of the contents. Going a little farther along in the tide streak I found another case. I put rope slings on and hoisted it on deck. In moving along the streak we found these cases quite plenty. Having a small crew, it was hard, slow work getting them on board. As I looked towards Wood Island I saw several fishing schooners standing out in the tide streak, some two miles to the south of me. In a short time they had all their boats out, probably towing cases to the schooners, to be hoisted on board. About three o'clock in the afternoon the wind died away so I could not follow up the tide streak. I could see the small boats apparently busy, to the south of me, until sunset. I had my pilot boat deck about full of cases, and I started for home. The wind being light and ahead, we arrived home the next day about noon.

THE ADVANTAGE OF KNOWING MR. FARMER.— I reported to Mr. J. L. Farmer what I had picked up eight or ten miles to sea. He told me to put them into the Grand Trunk sheds. I asked him if he would receipt for them. He said no, but told me to put them into the shed and they would be all right; but that did not suit me, as I knew Mr. Farmer. I called on Captain Sargent, the Custom House boarding officer, and told him that I had seen Mr. Farmer and he would not receipt for the goods. Captain Sargent said he could not sign for them.

I told him the steamship "St. George" was due here that night to take the mails to Liverpool, in the place of the ship "Bohemian," and when she came in my boat would be back with the goods. I lashed them so they would be safe in case of rough weather, went out for the ship "St. George," and got her about midnight. In the morning my boat came in. On seeing Captain Sargent he told me that after I went outside, Mr. Farmer called on him and wished him to send the cutter out and get the goods that Captain Willard had taken in his pilot boat, as he thought that the heat from the cook stove would injure them. Captain Sargent told him that he saw Willard before he went out, and the boat would be in by morning as the steamer was due here that evening. When the boat arrived I put the goods in charge of the United States Marshal, and they were discharged at Portland Pier, at E. Churchill's Iron Block.

Many fishermen put their goods into the Grand Trunk Railroad sheds. I learned they did not get one cent salvage for them. When the matter was settled, my part and the pilot boat netted me $800, and my crew made good day pay, as their shares were fixed as law fixes such cases. After that a wrecking company from St. John, N. B., was hired to save the cargo on percentage, I learned. I was there often, when out looking for jobs, to see the divers work.

ASLEEP ON THE BOTTOM OF THE SEA.—One day the diver went down and sent up several slings of pig iron. After that the man attending the life-line got no signal, but did not dare to pull up for fear of fouling the diver in the wreck. Mr. Dennis, the boss, thought something was wrong, so he hurriedly put on his suit, started another air-pump, and went down and gave signals to haul up the diver. The men in the boat felt that something must be wrong, and when they got him up to the boat and took off his face-piece he waked up. He had fallen asleep, and as the air-pumps were going he got a comfortable nap down on the bottom of the sea. Some said he was out late the night before, and it was hinted that he occasionally took strong tea.

ONE OF SPOT'S TRICKS.

CHAPTER XI.

DEEP-SEA FISHING.—THE NERVOUS MAN AND HIS GUN.—CAPTURING A DUSKY SHARK.—THE ADVENTURE OF THE SCOTCHMAN AND THE WHALE.—MY TRAINED PETS, THE COACH DOG AND THE CEDAR BIRD.

THE season of 1864 was good for deep-sea fishing. We got three or four sword-fish and one blackfish. While out looking for ships I could see where the game was bedded thick, and would make up a party of friends to enjoy the sport. One of these parties consisted of George Trefethen, Charles, Henry, and Alpheus Sterling, myself, and Mr. J., one of the most excitable men I ever knew. On this account we gave him the front berth. His weapon was a double-barreled shot gun, muzzle loader, such as we all used in those days. Sometimes he would get two charges of shot in one barrel and two of powder in the other, so that the first would not go off and the second would not kill. At Half Way Rock there was plenty of game, no light-house being there to frighten it off. Frequently when out for ships I have seen gunners there when the mercury would be twelve below zero, and have carried hot coffee ashore to them—a much more comforting drink on a cold morning than Sebago. On the fishing trips I had very good luck, striking some big game, but never was it my fortune to find the much-talked-of sea serpent, which has been so frequently seen, under favorable conditions, by excited sportsmen and tourists on the Cape Elizabeth shore. Once, however, I sailed many miles for him, as I will presently relate.

DUSKY MANEATER SHARK, 12 FEET LONG. 7 FEET GIRT.

CAPTURING A DUSKY SHARK.—During the summer of 1864 I took a party of ladies and gentlemen on a deep-sea-fishing trip, when we struck bigger game than we had counted on. We hove to on Rock Cod Ledge, where we found the cod-fish quite plenty. The day was delightful, the water perfectly smooth, and nobody seasick. After dinner we stood off shore some ten or twelve miles, hoping to see a sword-fish; but meeting with no luck started for home. On the way back I saw a ripple from the fin of a big fish, and tacked round and ran for him. The fin did not show enough to indicate his species. As we got near he began to sink slowly in the water, so I hastened to use the harpoon, striking him solid before its staff was out of sight. Then I gave him a hundred fathoms of line with a half barrel tied on the end, and sailed around for a short time in search of other fish. Finding none I took my boat with one of the crew, picked up the barrel, and pulled in the fish. The line was coiled carefully in a tub so as to run clear in case he proved game. Several times we got him near the boat, and then he would make for the bottom. By his action I judged he was a sword-fish. When he grew tired we pulled him to the boat, and to my great astonishment he proved a big, man-eating shark. Then I tried to get my harpoon out and let him go, having no fancy to bother with the creature; but it was in too deep. I would not cut the line, for it was my favorite harpoon and rarely failed me. When he was got along-side the pilot boat all the sails were lowered in order that the halyards might be used to hoist him in with. We got slings on him, but he slipped out, and I jumped for the lance. While lancing him the blood colored the water all about, and one of the ladies seized me by the arm and exclaimed, "Oh, captain! Don't! You will hurt him!"

HEAD TRICK.

I told her I guessed she had never been out a-sharking before.

When the fish became quiet we hoisted him on deck. He listed the boat a foot or more. He measured twelve feet in length, girt seven, his liver filled a barrel, and he had seven rows of teeth — the outside ones very large and about two inches long.

The shark was put on exhibition in a fish market for two days, and a large number of people called to see it. Mr. Charles Fuller, the naturalist, said that it was a dusky shark, whose habit is the Pacific Ocean. It was the only one ever captured on this coast. After we were done exhibiting it we gave it as a present to the Portland Natural History Society to be mounted. It was burned at the time of the big fire.

In the summer of 1865 we went on a sword-fishing trip off Monhegan Island. The following comprised the party: Mr. Lemuel Cushing, owner of Cushing's Island; Edward Bicknell, Salem, Mass.; Edward Keene, John Bradford, Capt. J. Blake, and others. We captured seven sword-fish and one shark and were three days on the trip. On another sword-fishing trip, a few days later, were the following party: John H. Fogg, Lemuel Cushing, Edward Keene, Capt. James Blake, and four others. We captured thirteen sword-fish, on a three and a half days' trip.

In August, 1865, I went to Portsmouth to pilot the United States monitor "Dictator," Admiral Farragut and Commodore Bailey. The United States monitor "Agamenticus" accompanied her to Portland. The two monitors had a sharp race from Portsmouth to Portland, the "Dictator" being beaten about two miles, owing to her bearings heating up.

THE SCOTCHMAN AND THE WHALE.—About this

CAPTAIN WILLARD AND HIS DOG SPOT.

time a Scotch whaler was introduced to me who wished to go out. He had been on several trips in a New Bedford whaler, and said that he could put me on to a whale. I told him if he could I would do the harpooning. The first day we saw nothing. It blew up to the south and we harbored at Wood Island for the night. In the morning we stood out towards Jeffery's Bank. We caught all the cod and mackerel we wanted, and soon saw a whale. The boat was manned and supplied with implements, provisions, and water. When we got near to the whale, he came up and blowed and went down to sound. The crew were ordered to peak their oars and wait until he came up again. The Scotchman thought the whale like a sperm whale, which would come up where he went down; but when he came up he was a good half-mile distant. We were rowing nearly all of the forenoon, and I did not see that my Scotch friend could get any nearer the whale than I could. About noon it breezed up to the south, so we abandoned the chase and went aboard to dinner. After dinner we resumed the pursuit in the "Nettle" and saw a school of blackfish four or five miles in length. We ran for them, but before reaching the spot saw a large whale, which seemed to be bothered by the many fish about him. He stayed on top of the water most of the time. It seemed a good chance to iron him before he saw us, but before we got near enough he took the alarm and got out of the way. However, I had the good fortune to harpoon a blackfish crossing the bow.

Presently we sighted another whale. I had on board a whale gun to shoot explosive lances. The barrel was made by Charles E. Staples & Son, Commercial Street, and it was stocked by Gilbert L. Bailey,

CAPTAIN WILLARD BATTLING WITH A WHALE.

Middle Street. When using a harpoon or gun I would stand on the end of the bowsprit with a line around my body and jibstay so as not to lose my balance. A short line was attached to the gun so it should not be lost overboard. This time we could not get close enough to the whale to blow him up, and, as the water was growing rough, abandoned the attempt. I passed the gun over to the Scotchman, but he lost his balance as he grasped it, and tumbled overboard with the weapon in his hand. Fortunately he caught hold of the whale line, though in so doing he was forced to drop the gun, and Mr. William Taylor grasped him by the collar as soon as his head was out of the water. When we pulled him aboard the first words he said were:

"Captain, I have lost your gun, and I am sorry."

I told him that I didn't mind the gun as long as we had got him. He was the coolest man I ever saw go overboard, and a comical fellow, too, always saying quaint things that kept the company in a merry mood. Among the party who witnessed his mishap were W. Taylor, Edward Bicknell, of Salem, Mass., Benjamin W. Nason and George H. Estes, of Durham, Me., and Capt. James Blake.

August and September, 1865, were fine months for mackereling. I went on several trips, taking on the first occasion Messrs. Charles J. Pennell, Edward Bicknell, Edward Keene, Capt. James Blake, B. F. Willard, and one or two others whose names I do not now recall. The mackerel were large and fat, and I salted enough to last my family all winter.

My Trained Pets. — In the spring of 1866 the captain of a British brig, loaded with molasses from Matanzas, brought back with him a black and white

DOG AND BIRD TRICK.

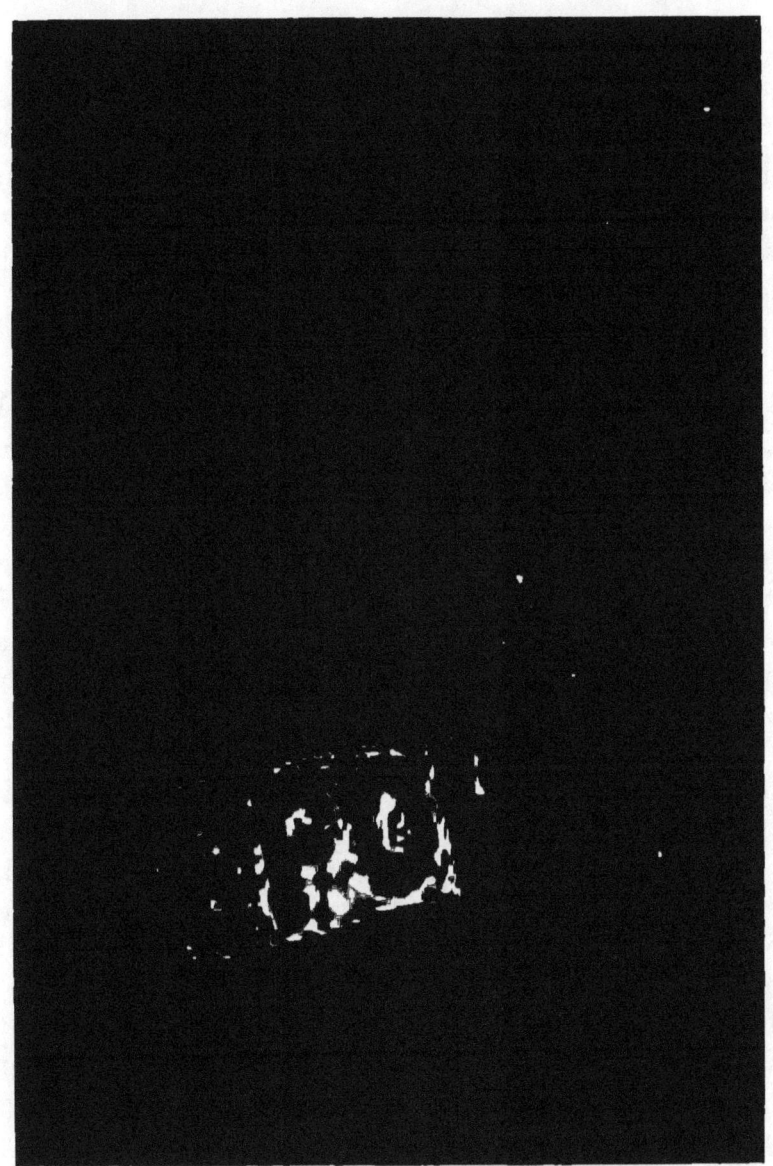

SPOT SPELLING HIS NAME.

spotted, full-blooded Spanish coach pup as a pet for his children, who were on board. Not wishing to take the dog across to England he gave him to me, and I put him in charge of O. B. Muller for training during the summer while I was yachting. The pup was quick to learn and of a most docile disposition. Muller taught him seven tricks. Then I took him in the fall and kept on training him until he could perform fifty-five. I treated him kindly and never had to whip him. I taught him in six evenings, without a motion of the whip, to spell his name by taking the letters out of the alphabet. Calling the letter I wanted, he would take it out of the row and bring it to me, and never make a mistake. When I left the city for eight or ten days I would tell him to stay with Mr. Muller, and he was never known to go upstairs to my room while I was away. I could send him with any stranger by telling him to go, and had no trouble in taking him to a photograph gallery, where he was pictured doing all his tricks on the first trial.

A friend of mine gave me a native cedar bird, commonly called a cherry bird. I took him out of the cage and trained him in twenty minutes to stand still on the dog's head and eat sugar out of my hand. Mr. Edward Woodbury, of Cape Elizabeth, was present at the time. Finally I had a cap and perch made to fit the dog's head, with an elastic underneath his chin to hold it, so the bird could stand firm on the perch while the dog was performing. But one thing that I could never teach him to do was to fly from the dog's head to his cage. I suppose that he did not exercise his wings enough to strengthen them. The dog never offered to harm the bird. They seemed to be happy in performing together. They were both trained by kind

DOG AND BIRD TRICK.

CHAIR TRICK.

treatment. I had the bird three or four years, and he died and I had him mounted and put into my cabinet with my other curiosities.

I have been offered large sums of money for the dog, one man in Toronto, Canada, offering me $500. I told him that was worth five hundred dogs, but I was so attached to my pet I could not think of selling him. After seeing the dog perform, the Toronto man said probably he would not do it for anybody else. Though never having tried it, I thought the dog would. I told my visitor to take my whip, and stood behind him and instructed him what to do; telling him to drag the whip on the floor, walk back slowly, call the dog by name, and tell him to creep. The dog did so immediately. Then the whip was swung cross-way and the dog told to sit up. He did so at once. Many other tricks were also performed, much to the Canadian man's delight. After having the dog fifteen years, he became blind, and I got Doctor Bailey to chloroform him. I had him buried on my lot in the cemetery at Cape Elizabeth, with a fifty-dollar head-stone on which he is carved in the act of performing one of his tricks. The accompanying illustrations will convey a good idea of the dog and bird while going through some of their performances.

CHAPTER XII.

A WHALE IN THE HARBOR. — THE SEVEN TON BLACKFISH. — HOW A HAYSEED SPOILED HIS LINEN TROUSERS. — APPEARANCE AND HABITS OF THE BLACKFISH. — A LIVELY FIGHT WITH A SWORD-FISH. — THE SUMMER OF 1867.

IN July, 1866, an unexpected visitor, a whale, came into the harbor. As soon as I received the news I got the following men: A. Taylor, Chas. Harris, John Shaw, C. Burns, and A. H. Mantine. We went to the pilot boat "Nettle," got whale line, harpoons, lances, and whale gun to shoot bomb lances and blow him up if we could not get near enough to harpoon. We started out and struck him once, but in a few minutes the harpoon drew out. Then we loaded the whale gun. We were near Vaughan's Bridge, which was full of teams and people, while all the shores were filled with anxious spectators. Shortly he came up to blow within fifteen yards of us; but was side to, his back some two feet above the water. I aimed the gun near the edge of the water and fired the bomb lance. It went through his back, skipped some twenty feet or more on the water, and burst, making the water fly high in the air. This enraged him and he went fast for the railroad bridge. When near it he would find the piling thick, then change his course across the channel. When passing the draw the water was thick with mud that he had stirred up. He could not see the draw, and as he came down ran on to the old ways left there after one of the gunboats was launched. Nearly half his back was out of the water. We in the boat saw his

BLACK FISH.
Length 24 ft. — Girth 14 ft. Weight about 14,000 lbs.

position, and rowed with all our strength to get to him before he could back off. Being flood tide, before we could get near enough to iron him he ran from one bridge to another, saw the wide space in the draw, and went through it. When he got to Portland Bridge he passed through some distance south of the draw, and we saw him no more. He was a young whale, some thirty feet in length. If we had thought to set a net across the draw we could have kept him there until the next low water. I guess the whale came upon an excursion to view the ruins of Portland, for it was just after the big fire.

A few days later a captain of a fishing schooner informed me that he saw several sword-fish twenty-five miles southeast of Cape Elizabeth. I got the following crew: Capt. Scott B. Oliver, Capt. William Small, Capt. William Senter, Capt. James Blake, and two others, went out to the place reported and found them. We got seven large fish and were back the same evening.

A SEVEN-TON BLACKFISH.—Shortly after I went on a blackfish trip with the following crew: Capt. K. D. Atwood, Mr. Theophilus Hopkins, Isaac Smith, Capt. James Blake, and some others. When about twenty miles south southeast from Cape Elizabeth lights, we sighted a large school of blackfish, some three miles in length, and sailed for them. I was on the end of the bowsprit as a big blackfish came up to blow. It was a long distance to harpoon, but I sent it some thirty feet and hit him hard. When we hauled him along-side, Atwood asked me what I would do with him. I said hoist him on board. We put the fore-throat halyards on him, but could not hoist the head half out of the water. Then the question came how to tow him. If tail foremost we would be a long time in getting him in. So we put the anchor rope fast to the tail, led it to the head, lashed it, put old canvas on the rope to save the chaffing and towed him head foremost. During this time the wind changed to northwest with a fresh breeze and we were some twenty miles to leeward of Cape Elizabeth. The first tack we fetched Seguin Island, and, the wind favoring us, on the next tack, Trundy's Reef buoy. We arrived at the Custom House dock near dark. After supper I had twenty men to help me hoist the fish up, and put him into Yeaton & Smith's market, at Main Wharf, where he was to be exhibited. It was low water, and when most up to the top of the wharf he slipped out of the slings and went down, making a big splash. Then we slung him solid and bridled him from head to tail. When up to the cap of the wharf again, one of the shear legs broke, and down he went the second time. We thought the shears were good for more than his weight, but we had under-estimated him, thinking he would weigh eight or ten thousand pounds, instead of seven tons as it proved. Then we went to Franklin Wharf, got large spars, and rigged up again. By this time it was midnight, and down came fifteen policemen, who took hold of the fall, which was a luff tackle, and up he went. Then came hard work to haul him into the market with another large tackle. When we got him in there we put the tape on, and he measured twenty-four feet in length and twelve feet in circumference.

AN UNBELIEVER AND HIS LINEN TROUSERS.— We had him on exhibition two days, and the market was filled with people the most of the time. The last day he swelled up large, the result of which was some fun. A man and a boy came from the country, both wearing linen trousers. The old man said it was a humbug; that it was India rubber blown up, and not a fish. I showed him where the skin was off and he could see the blubber, but to no purpose. He went around where the harpoon was imbedded. I left it there so the people could see where the fish was hit. The old man asked what that was. I told him it was the harpoon that captured the fish. He took hold of it. I told him to be careful or he might get something on him that wouldn't smell good. At that moment he gave a jerk as if he were mad. The matter came out as if out of a gun, and he and the boy got the full force on their new linen trousers. The last I saw of them they were on the wharf working with straw to clean the filth from their clothes. The smell was worse than porgy oil. The blubber of the fish was taken off and the oil tried out by John Stillwell, the whaler, and put into barrels over night. The barrels shrunk up during the night and we lost about one hundred dollars' worth of oil. The dock in the morning was covered with it. The oil was sold, and what was taken at the exhibition amounted to $350. The crew shared about $70 apiece. The carcass was given to a farmer to haul off, and we had lots of sport with him. When the harpoon was cut out it was within two or three inches of the heart.

The blackfish is a true cetacean (delphinus globiceps, Cuvier) and is commonly called the social bottle head or howling whale. Although having a fish-like form it is, as the other cetaceans, not a fish but a true air-breathing mammal, warm blooded, bringing forth its young alive, and suckling them for a considerable period. The manner in which nature works its transformation from one order of beings to another is curiously illustrated in the pectoral fins of the blackfish, which are in reality the forelegs of the animal, containing the usual bones of the vertebrate arm. Being an air-breathing animal, thrown into the sea to live among the fishes, it is thus adapted to its home by having its anterior limbs converted into powerful fins. The posterior limbs are dispensed with, the only trace of them being a pair of pelvic bones suspended among the muscles and detached from the spine. The blackfish is remarkable for its social disposition, herding together in great numbers. This specimen as it lay upon its belly measured five feet from the back to the top of its dorsal fin. Its shape was like that of two inclined planes united in a crest or dorsal fin. Its head was obtuse, conical, and rounded. Its mouth was comparatively small, with teeth set wide apart, and about half an inch long. Its nostrils opened on the top of the head, and like that of the whale constituted the blow holes for purposes of respiration and the expulsion of water, not for the exercise of smell. There were no external ears, and the eyes were small, not larger than those of an ox, and apparently very far back. Its skin was without scales, perfectly smooth, black in color, and very much resembling India rubber in appearance. The head was disproportionately large, the body tapering rapidly from the dorsal fin to the tail, which had two flukes extended horizontally. These flukes the animal, in propelling itself through the water, bends into the exact form of a propeller. It was doubtless from this that our inventors got their idea of the steam propeller. The blackfish like all the cetaceans is carnivorous, preying on smaller fish, like mackerel or herring, opening his mouth and swallowing numbers as he drives through the frightened schools of small fry. The oil is clear, and as nice as sperm oil.

A Fight with a Sword-Fish.—In the summer of 1867 we went on several sword-fishing trips and had a hard fight with one fish about twenty miles from Cape Elizabeth. At the time we were laying becalmed and we sighted a big fish a short distance away.

Mr. Henry M. Turner was one of the party and I took him in the boat to scull me. I harpooned the fish, and when he was hit it numbed him. We backed off some forty or fifty fathoms of line from him. He came up and took a circle, and, when half-way around again, came straight for us. I told Turner to keep the boat head on to him, and when he got near the bow I shoved the lance in him up to the socket. That seemed to still him for a while and the speed carried him under the boat. I told Turner to back off immediately. This time we backed the whole length of the line, one hundred fathoms. Just as the line came taut the fish rose to the top of the water, circled around as he did at first, and came for us again. I waited until he got near enough for me to shove the lance into him. When I did so, and put my weight on it, the dory slewed, he put his head up, and the sword came up over the gunwale. I told Turner to catch him by the sword. He did so with both hands. The fish remained quiet, probably for fear of breaking his sword. I made good use of the lance while he was in this position, lanced him several times, and then as he was sinking told Turner to let go and back off. We backed off the whole length of the line, and kept it taut so as to know his position. I concluded that he could not stand it long and as he did not come on top of the water again, I concluded that he must be dead and on the bottom. After waiting some twenty to thirty minutes we hauled him up from the bottom in about fifty fathoms of water.

The party on the pilot boat felt very anxious about us after seeing such a battle, but they had no wind to get to us. We put a tail rope on him and towed him to the pilot boat. He proved to be fifteen feet long and weighed four hundred pounds.

I consider it very dangerous to have slack line after making fast to a sword-fish, as you do not know what minute he will come up through the bottom of the boat. By backing off and keeping a taut line you can tell just where he is. One time I struck a small sword-fish off the bowsprit of the "Nettle." She was going at eight or nine knots with a strong breeze. The fish was heading the same way the boat was. He turned around quickly and ran into the pilot boat abaft the main rigging, ran his sword through the waist-board and into a white-oak timber some three inches and broke it off. It was lucky that his sword did not go above the rail, as the cockpit was full of people and some one might have been injured by it. A line and keg were thrown overboard and the boat hove to. Two of us took the dory, picked up the buoy, and hauled on to him, coiling the rope into a tub. He was apparently dead and did not move. We hauled him up and put a tail line on him. The pilot boat came up to us and took a line. The fish was hauled along-side the boat and hoisted on board. He showed no sign of life. We were on our way home when we sighted him. When near Portland Head Light he came to life and went to jumping. One time I thought that he would go overboard before I could get him still. We stilled him by hitting him on his sword with a club.

CHAPTER XIII.

IN WHICH ALL MANNER OF FISH IS SOUGHT, FROM SEA SERPENT TO MACKEREL.—A FIGHT BETWEEN A SWORD-FISH AND TWO KILL-ERS.—ST. ELMO'S FIRE.—THE RACE BETWEEN THE "NETTLE" AND "SPARKLE."—A FAMOUS TROUTING PARTY ON MOUNT DESERT. CONCERNING WATER-SPOUTS.—HUNTING EIDER DUCKS. DOCTOR BOWLES AND THE WHITE TAILED MARTIN.—THE BEGINNING OF THE SWORD-FISH INDUSTRY.

JULY 25, 1867, the "Nettle" sailed on a deep-sea-fishing trip, well prepared to capture anything from a sea serpent down to a mackerel. When about twenty-five miles from Cape Elizabeth we saw something ahead, at times, making the water fly. The water was smooth, with a light southwest wind. As we neared the strange object we saw something black sticking up three or four feet. The party became very much excited and said that it must be the sea serpent. They asked me if I was going to harpoon him, and I said yes, I would harpoon anything in the water if I could get near enough. But, getting close to the suspicious thing, we found it to be two large killers having a terrific battle with a sword-fish. These fish were all of thirty feet in length, with a high fin on the back. We could see the sword-fish at times showing a fin and going through the water very fast. I thought that it would be a good chance to use my harpoon, but the eyes of the fish were too sharp for me. When we got close to them they would go down and come up in another direction. In a short time the killers seemed to be victorious, and the sword-fish took a northeast direction and left them, going faster than we could sail with a three-knot breeze. But before he got out of sight from the mast-head he turned around and began to circle, probably to see if the killers were after him. By this means we gained on him, got into good position, and harpooned him. After being fast to him for about an hour and a half we got him up to the boat and lanced him. His length was twelve feet, three inches. He was large in body and evidently a male fish. The male fish do the fighting and are provided with a solid sword. The female sword contains different cells the whole length. I have a female sword in my office sawed vertically, which is a curiosity to see.

SPORT OFF MONHEGAN AND SEGUIN.—After the fish was aboard we sailed for Monhegan Island. There we had grand good luck and sport. We captured five good-sized sword-fish and returned home, having been out only two days. The combined length of the five fish was sixty-eight feet, seven inches. In the party were Capt. James Blake, Alex Taylor, Lemuel Cushing, and several others whom I do not remember. On these trips I could only take four or five passengers besides my crew, on account of the small space for sleeping. All the party were highly pleased with the trip, and wished to go again. A great many wished to go, but there was not room enough to accommodate them. Oftentimes they would engage ahead so as to get the chance of going.

My next trip was a short one for a day to the south of Seguin Island. We caught one large sword-fish weighing nearly five hundred pounds, and a large sunfish nearly the same weight. On seeing a large whale, some fifty to sixty feet long, we tried to get on him for harpooning, but his eyes were too sharp for us. It is surprising how far whales can see, considering that their eyes are only as large as those of an ox. I loaded the whale gun with the bomb lance and took it on the end of the bowsprit, but the nearest that I could get was from twenty to thirty yards. The next time he came up to blow, heading from us, I fired the gun, aiming a little high. The bomb lance hit him on the back, glanced, and bounded some distance ahead. Before he had time to get up where it was it exploded. He changed his course, and made the water foam. It looked as though he was going fifty miles an hour, and it was only a short time before he was out of sight.

St. Elmo's Fire.—I have frequently mentioned St. Elmo's fire. There is a class of quite harmless phenomena caused by a strong degree of electricity, where the air is highly charged, as during storms of snow or rain. These sometimes become visible in the form of pale-colored flames, quivering on the points of non-conductors or of insulated conductors. Mariner's lights, or St. Elmo's fire, is a phenomenon of this description, usually reckoned by sailors a fortunate omen. It was noticed during the voyages of Columbus and Magellan. Forbin thus describes its appearance as observed by him in 1696: "The sky was suddenly covered with thick clouds. Fearing a gale, I had all the sails reefed. There were more than thirty St. Elmo's fires on the ship. One of them occupied the vane of the mainmast and was about nineteen inches long. I sent a sailor to fetch it. When he was aloft he heard a noise like that which is made when moist gunpowder is burned. I ordered him to take off the vane. He had scarcely executed this order when the fire quitted it and placed itself at the top of the mainmast, whence it could not possibly be removed."

Admiral Smith describes one observed by him in

ST. ELMO'S FIRE.

1807, while on board the frigate "Cornwallis," in the Bay of Panama, of such brilliancy that they could see each other's faces on deck. I never saw any of these lights, but am acquainted with several captains who have seen them. I put this in, thinking it will be of interest to my readers.

THE "NETTLE" AND THE "SPARKLE."—Capt. William Senter owned a yacht named the "Sparkle." Being about the size of my boat (the "Nettle") and well matched for speed, we were often in the same company on shooting excursions and sailing parties. One memorable trip was from Portland to Bar Harbor. The "Sparkle" had a party of ten and crew and the "Nettle" the same. We sailed from Portland in the forenoon in a strong southwest wind. My pilot was to take us to Bass Harbor; then their pilot was to take charge from there to Bar Harbor. The first night was spent at Herring Gut. We got under way in the morning with a fair wind as strong as we wished. Mr. Senter was trying his best to pass the "Nettle," but when he got on the weather quarter she gradually dropped astern. Then he changed his course to the leeward of our wake, so she would come up slowly and get near enough to enable each party to talk and toss boiled eggs to and fro. When we arrived at Bass Harbor bar, I luffed into the wind and let the "Sparkle" take the lead; then I tried my best for the rest of the day to pass by her, watching strong flaws of wind to get my jib far enough ahead to take the wind out of her mainsail so I could pass. In so doing I dropped slowly astern; then changed my course to the leeward of her wake and gained until we could easily converse with each other. We went in this wise all the way to Bar Harbor, arriving there near night. Both yachts luffed up and anchored simultaneously, making fourteen hours running time, which was very good for small yachts. My party consisted of Judge Edward Fox, Rev. Dr. Burgess, Rev. Dr. Shailer, George E. B. Jackson, and others. I don't remember the date of this trip, but think there were only two boarding-houses at Bar Harbor then.

A TROUTING TRIP AT BAR HARBOR.—We learned that some of the "Sparkle" party were going trouting in the morning. One of them was Lieutenant Inman, who had been there before. He had written ahead and engaged the only boat they had in the trout pond. As Messrs. Burgess and Jackson felt sorry that they could not go trouting too, I told them that I thought it could be arranged. I went ashore and saw a farmer and engaged him to take his hay-rack and haul my boat to the pond, which was some four miles away. Several of each party stopped ashore nights. In the morning while they were at breakfast I dug angle worms for bait. The boat was put on hay so as to ride easy. The morning being misty, we took our rubber coats and started for the pond. We arrived at the foot, put our boat into the water, and got the farmer to come back for us late in the afternoon. Rowing up to the head of the pond we found our foresighted friends, who were very much surprised to see us. They were having fine luck, catching trout fast, and were mighty proud of a fancy dip net they had brought along. We anchored there and began to fish. The mist cleared, giving us a good overcast day, and the trout bit fast. Mr. Burgess said it was a pity we did not have a dip net for them. In a few minutes he hooked a good-sized trout. I took Judge Fox's sou'wester hat to use as a dip net and it worked like a charm. The trout ran into it and I made quite a haul, spattering Mr. Burgess in the operation. However, he did not mind that as long as we got the fish and beat the other fellows. We caught all the trout that we wanted, and put some in the ice-chest so we had them fresh all the rest of the trip. I split, salted, and dried some of them. When dried they were as tough as leather and had no taste.

WATER-SPOUTS. — Having been asked to describe water-spouts, I insert this short description. Water-spouts are whirlwinds occurring on the sea or on lakes. They first appear in the form of an inverted cone attached to a dark cloud. The cone swings backwards and forwards, and gradually approaches the water, which becomes violently agitated. The whirling eddy draws up masses of spray which unite with the descending cone. When fully formed they appear as tall pillars of clouds of a sombre gray, stretching from the sea to the sky, whirling around on their axes. Besides this rotary, they have a progressive, motion. They continue but a brief time, when the column breaks, and rain often descends from the clouds above. The drops of water forming this rain are never salt, as would be the case were they carried up from the ocean. They must be derived from the clouds, as is ordinary rain. The accompanying illustration gives a good idea of them.

A FRUITLESS HUNT FOR EIDER DUCKS. — In the winter of 1868 the sea game were very plentiful, particularly the eider ducks, whose places of feeding were Green Island Reefs and Half Way Rock. They came in thousands. I got up the following party to go to Half Way Rock: William Senter, George, Henry, and Charles Trefethen, and Alpheus Sterling. The wind was northwest, and blowing very heavy and cold. We

WATER-SPOUTS.

ran outside of Bangs Island and anchored under the lee to get an early start for the shooting grounds. We got under way early in the morning, but found we could not steer the boat as the rudder had frozen up solid in the rudder port. We had to haul down the head sail and heat water to thaw it out. The thermometer was twelve below zero. When passing Green Island it came on to blow a gale. We stood in under the lee of Jewell's Island and anchored, hoping to see the wind die away so we could have some fun with the ducks. We found after breakfast that the wind kept on blowing and we decided to come home with no ducks that trip.

MR. BOWLES AND THE WHITE-TAILED MARTIN.—In May we had a fine gunning trip to Cape Small Point. We got some over two hundred game, mostly of the coot kind. We had gray coot, white-winged coot, butter-bill coot, old squaw, some wild pigeon, a few northern divers, one fine comorant, and one large white-tailed martin. The party consisted of Jonas Hamilton, George Trefethen, J. N. Martin, Mr. Taylor, William Senter, myself, and two others. On the way home we took one morning at Hussey's Sound for old squaws. Hamilton and Trefethen being the last to leave the pilot boat, they hove fifteen or twenty old squaws aboard, and started for the sound to shoot. About 10 A. M. all the shooters came on board. Some of the boats had from five to seven. Hamilton and Trefethen began to throw theirs out and count them, and all the rest of the shooters were very much surprised to see so many birds with so little shooting. On arriving at Portland the birds fell short in number. Then it leaked out that they took a supply in the morning from the pilot boat.

The next morning a list of our game was in the daily papers. The Rev. Mr. Bowles, seeing the list of game, called on Mr. Trefethen and asked him what he did with the comorant. He told him that Willard hove him overboard. Mr. Bowles said he was very sorry for that, as it was a rare bird on this coast and he wanted it to mount for the Natural History Society. He saw by the paper that we had one large white-tailed martin. Trefethen explained that the rare bird was Mr. Martin, and said that Willard shot Martin with a number four spent shot. It stung him on the cheek, but did not break the skin, as the distance was some two hundred yards.

In the morning Mr. Hamilton saw the same account in the papers, and called on Martin at the roundhouse, saying that the Rev. Mr. Bowles wanted to see him.

"What does he want to see me for?" innocently asked Mr. Martin.

Hamilton said, "He wants to get your hide to mount for the Natural History Society."

"What are you coming at?" said Martin.

Hamilton then asked him if he hadn't seen the paper that morning. When it was handed to him and he read the remarkable item of news his wrath was only equaled by his astonishment.

MAKING A BIG HAUL OF SWORD-FISH.—During the summer of 1868, the sword-fish were very plentiful and I captured sixty-four of them. My largest trip I brought in August 27th. I had seventeen sword-fish and one shark. One of these fish was twenty-one feet in length, and weighed nine hundred and fifty-nine pounds. The smallest one was eleven feet long. This one, with the shark, was given to the Peabody Institute to be mounted. The trip lasted three days. The following composed the party: Capt. A. S. Oliver, Capt. James Blake, Edward Keene, Lemuel Cushing, Edwin Bicknell, of Salem, Mass, and one or two others. We saw no one else fishing on the grounds. These fish were caught twenty-five miles south southeast of Monhegan Island.

My next sword-fish trip was to the same grounds. We found plenty of them and captured twelve in one day; then hove to for the night. During the first part of the night we were busy dressing the sword-fish to ice up. It being calm and smooth, the sharks came around in great numbers to get the waste we were throwing overboard. While washing the deck down one came up to the scupper to get the blood that was running out, and the top of his back was out of the water. I told the party to stand back away from his tail and I would lance him. I took the lance and stood on the house away from the rail, giving it to him good and hard. In his hurry to get away from the boat his tail came out of the water five or six feet, throwing water nearly all over the boat. No sooner was that shark driven off than others came up to the same place. I lanced three or four more for the amusement of the party. When morning came the wind began to breeze up southeast and rain to fall. It came a strong gale and we had to run for home. The seventeen sword-fish lot brought eight and a half cents a pound, the twevle lot eight and a quarter. They were shipped to Boston by K. D. Atwood. During the summer I stocked $1,150 on sword-fish. Then all the fishermen prepared for sword-fishing, and have made a business of it ever since.

CHAPTER XIV.

A CRUISE FOR THE SEA SERPENT. — DISTINGUISHED JURISTS AND CLERGYMEN HUNTING THE WHALE. — LOTS OF FUN BUT NO FISH. — A COLORED COOK WHO TURNED WHITE. — COLLECTING SHIP NEWS FOR THE DAILY PAPERS. — RESCUE OF A GUNNING PARTY ON HALF WAY ROCK. — CAPTAIN SEXTER AND THE "SPARKLE."

ABOUT this time a sea serpent was reported off the coast. I got a crew and started in the "Nettle" in search. We cruised three days without seeing him, and then abandoned the quest. On the way back we captured a blackfish and sold it to Mr. Johnson, the lobster dealer, thus making more out of our hunt than most people do who chase sea serpents.

In the spring of 1869 the "Nettle" and the "Sparkle" both took gunning parties to Cape Small Point Harbor and gunned in the small boats. Later in the season I took the following party for deep-sea fishing: Judge Edward Fox, Rev. Dr. Shailer, Rev. Dr. Burgess, George E. B. Jackson, Mr. John Short, Capt. James Blake, Dixon D. Fuller, and two others besides the crew. When about a mile outside Ram Island, Judge Fox saw a big fish break water and called my attention to it. After a few minutes we saw a young whale some thirty feet in length come up and blow. I immediately got my harpoon ready and took position on the end of the bowsprit, with a life-line around my body and jibstay. Fuller hauled the boat up and got things ready. At that moment the whale blew close to the lee quarter. As he came forward I could see him under water. He crossed under the bowsprit, some ten feet deep, and came up on the starboard side to blow, giving me a good chance to throw it with all my might and it took effect about midway on the left side and buried all of two feet in him. I told Fuller to jump into the boat with another man, and got in off the bowsprit as soon as possible. As I boarded the boat the whale began to run the line quickly out of the tub, and the man who got in with Fuller grew frightened, jumping out, and climbed upon the yacht. We gave the fish the whole line of a hundred fathoms in order to get the end through a leader in the bow of the boat. The boat was only fourteen feet long, built sharp for a stevedore boat, and unsuitable to attack large fish in. The whale ran to the southwest until he got in the ship channel; then changed his course to northwest and ran for Portland Harbor. We had hauled in about fifty fathoms of line, and when opposite Portland Head Light he came up to blow and then went under; heaving his tail up as they usually do when going down to sound. The next time he came up to blow I sent the lance into his back, but too far aft to be much good. At this time we were very near the yacht, thus giving the party a grand view of the monster. As he ran he kept near the top of the water, the line cutting through the water and humming like a fiddle-string, while every timber of the boat trembled. I really think that he was going thirty miles an hour.

"By jinks, aint he going?" shouted Fuller.

It being perfectly smooth water, we held to him. He only ran with this speed about ten minutes. We looked around to the pilot boat and she was four or five miles away, to the leeward, so we could hope for no help from her. Every time we hauled on to him and got near his tail, hoping to have a chance to lance him when he came up to blow, he would see us and run around in a circle with great speed, like a horse in a circus ring. Our boat being sharp, we could not turn around quick enough and would have to pay out line to keep from hauling under. The circling was repeated twenty-five or thirty times while we were fast to him. When to the south of Cape Elizabeth some six or seven miles, we came across Ellis Usher and took him on board, dropping his boat astern and towing her. Then I had help to haul on the line. But the two boats towing did not make any difference in the whale's speed. Several times I lanced him, but it was too far aft to be any good. When we had been fast to him about four hours he seemed to get tired, and as he came up to blow I sent the lance on an angle well forward. It took effect in his back about ten feet abaft the spout hole. The staff broke off at the socket. Then we were crippled, as it was all the lance we had in the boat. For about an hour the lance stayed there, showing the socket every time he came up to blow. Finally it worked itself out. We still held on to him, hoping that the pilot boat would get up to us so we could obtain some weapons. We could then have killed him easily. After being fast to him for six or seven hours the harpoon drew out. At this time we were about twenty-five miles south southeast of Cape Elizabeth, with the pilot boat all of six miles to our leeward. Then, being tired and hungry and with not a dry stitch on us, we gave up the chase.

Some two days after this the whale was picked up near Cape Small Point, towed in, and put on exhibition. When found by the fishermen he had a big wound midway on the left side and several wounds on the back.

He evidently died from what the doctors call heart failure, consequent upon the harpooning we gave him. It was my usual fortune with whales. I have had good luck in catching all other kinds of large fish, but whales have baffled me. I have been fast to several, but never succeeded in capturing one. However, the party enjoyed the sport hugely, and Judge Fox and his friends went on many a trip with me while I kept the "Nettle."

How the Black Cook Turned White.—The next trip out for big fishing I had no party excepting Capt. James Blake, a colored cook, and myself. We were some twenty-five miles south of Cape Elizabeth, when we saw a large school of blackfish, ran on to them, harpooned one of a good size, and took the line in the boat. I took the cook with me. The blackfish kept up with the school, towing fast. We hauled up to him and when he came up to blow I gave him the lance. Then he made the water fly high up in the air. I looked around to see if the cook was steering the boat and found he had turned white with fright. He begged me to cut the line and let the fish go. I told him when I got a little nearer I could kill it in a few minutes. We found that the fish would tow us up to Boon Island, so we hauled him roughly, to stop his speed, and the harpoon drew out. I think the cook was glad the fish got away, for he came to his natural color at once.

A Rescue at Half Way Rock.—When I first began stevedoring I collected ship news for the daily papers. While in the harbor one night a coaster came in, and reported that two gunners were on Half Way Rock, having lost their boat. He tried to rescue them, but the wind was blowing hard to the northwest and a rough sea raging, so he had to give up. They would freeze that night, he said, if not taken off. I went to the revenue cutter and reported the case to the lieutenant, who said he would send to the Cape for Captain Waldron. In the morning I was up to the Observatory before daylight. The cutter was getting under way to go down. One of the men on the rock was Douglas, the well-known gunner. Both were taken off by the cutter's boat in safety. They were Harpswell men, who went to Half Way Rock in a Hampton boat, and punt to land in. Some time in the day a heavy squall came up and the boat went adrift. They started in the punt to get the boat, but it upset and the two men swam ashore. The wind took the punt on shore so they turned it up on one side for shelter. They got some dry powder out of one of their powder horns and started a fire with what loose stuff they could gather. When that went out they ran to and fro over the rocks to keep warm. I don't see how they kept alive that bitter cold night with their clothing wet through. I have often thought of the night when I have been there with my friends on shooting trips. It will be seen by this that shooters on the water take chances; still it is not so dangerous as shooting in the woods, where gunners shoot on seeing the bushes move and often kill men in mistake for deer. I would rather trust myself on Half Way Rock than take to the bush with a careless man.

CAPTAIN SENTER AND THE "SPARKLE."—The fall of 1869 was good for sea game. Capt. William Senter and party with the yacht "Sparkle," and the pilot boat "Nettle" with a party, went to New Meadows Bay, had great sport, and shot a large number of surf ducks. Mr. Senter was the life of the company. When

CAPT. WILLIAM SENTER.

it was thick weather my lantern was put over the boat's stern by night to keep in sight with each other. At times the two parties would make bets on the first yacht to arrive and want me to help them. I said, "No, I never leave my friend Captain Senter in thick weather. If you had asked me before starting, I should have told you to never bet against Captain Senter and the yacht 'Sparkle.' His yacht and mine have taken many friendly parties out for shooting and deep-sea-fishing trips."

CHAPTER XV.

THE PEABODY OBSEQUIES. — ARRIVAL OF THE "MONARCH" OFF PORT LAND, AND SEVERE TRIP OF THE PILOT BOAT IN SEARCH OF HER.- THE IMPRESSIVE NAVAL PROCESSION UP THE HARBOR.— ADMIRAL FARRAGUT AND THE "TERROR." ANOTHER GREAT NAVAL PAGEANT.— THE DUKE OF NEWCASTLE'S HAT.

ON the 4th of November, 1869, the cable brought intelligence of the death of George Peabody, the eminent philanthropist, who, by the rare simplicity of his life, his upright and honorable career as a merchant, and his broad and liberal charities, had endeared himself to the English-speaking people of two continents.

It was his last wish that his body should repose in his native state, Massachusetts; and, so, after a stately funeral in Westminster Abbey, his remains were brought to America on the great iron-clad "Monarch," the pride of the British Navy, accompanied by American vessels of war, detailed as escort. Portland was designated as the landing place. By joint resolution of Congress the President of the United States was authorized to make suitable preparations for the reception of the body, and a fitting portion of our fleet ordered to repair to Portland under command of Admiral Farragut, the ranking officer of the American Navy. The "Miantonomah" and the "Terror" (formerly the "Agamenticus") were selected.

I was appointed pilot by the Board of Trade, in case such service should be required by the incoming fleet, and received my commission, signed by President Jonas H. Perley and Secretary M. N. Rich, on the 29th of December, 1869.

THE PEABODY FLEET ARRIVES.—January 25, 1870, I got a telegram saying that the "Monarch" and her escort, the "Plymouth," were off South Shoal light-ship. I got my boat ready, took the mails at the post-office directed to the two vessels, and put out to meet them. Reporters of the *New York Herald* and *Boston Globe*, who were lying in wait, called to get a chance to go on the pilot boat with me. I declined to take them, on the plea that I couldn't tell how long we should be out; but took Mr. L. H. Cobb, then of the *Portland Advertiser* and now editor of the *Press*. He was the only one I wished to take. My crew were Capt. William Small, Mr. Purington, and Mr. George Green, who was to pilot the "Plymouth" in. We started that afternoon, in a strong, northeast wind, with snow and sleet blowing. Three sails were carried.

When near Bangs Island I heard a gun at sea. At Ram Island Ledge we took in the foresail, as the sea was getting very rough. In sight of Bulwark Shoal it was breaking high. About that time a sharp, high comber came over the bow, tumbled down on deck, washed off the fore-scuttle hatch, and swept over the top of the house to the mainmast. Several barrels of water went down into the forecastle and struck a hot cook stove. Mr. Purington, who was in the cabin at the time, came running up and said that the bow was stove in. Captain Small at once put the hatch on and lashed it down, and I luffed up so the boat could shake the water off. When the steam cleared away so I could see the cabin the water was about two feet deep on the floor. It looked hard for a few minutes, but the only thing to do was to keep cool. The pumps were rigged and set to work, and after a time we surmounted the danger. Meanwhile we kept off for the ships, as we could hear their guns at constant intervals.

SIGHTING THE "MONARCH."—After passing Cod Ledge some two miles we sighted the "Monarch" in the mist, made toward her, and shortly saw the "Plymouth" a short distance to her leeward. We passed under the lee of the "Monarch" and hailed her to send a boat for the mail and pilot. Presently we got aboard, and the "Plymouth" being signaled, Mr. Green was sent to her as pilot. By this time the snow was quite thick, and the captain on the "Monarch" hesitated whether to go in or haul off for the night. On my assurance he went ahead, and anchored in the lower harbor.

Soon after we anchored, a government tug came along-side to render whatever assistance was needed. The captain of the "Monarch" wished me to see Admiral Farragut and ask him to take charge of the ship. This was about nine o'clock at night. I went ashore and found the Admiral at the Falmouth, where he made his quarters. The hotel corridors were filled with reporters and other curious people. The Admiral planned to have the ships come up the harbor, two abreast. On my reminding him how we sailed in the "Terror" (then the "Agamenticus") from Portsmouth some years before, and what a bad steering ship she was, he readily recalled the trip, and with a smile made his dispositions accordingly. About midnight he completed his preparations to go to the United States ships, and I was ordered to the "Monarch." When I went out to her in the morning on the government tug the reporters from New York and Boston wanted to go with me, and I took them. I was glad to show them the depth of water in Portland Harbor at low tide, as a bitter controversy had been raging between Boston and New York papers as to the respective depths of water in those harbors, each contending that a big battleship like the "Monarch" could not get into the waters of the other. The chance to show them the capacity of our harbor was too good to be missed.

When the "Monarch" came up the water was low, as it happened, and I called the attention of the reporters to that fact, inviting them to stand by the man who was heaving the sounding lead. The shoalest water we got all the way up was eight fathoms. They were much surprised at the depth and, I believe, made mention of the wonderful capabilities of Portland Harbor in their correspondence.

The "Monarch" was escorted up the harbor by the "Plymouth," "Miantonomah," and "Terror," and salutes repeatedly fired during the progress. By one of these discharges, in which sixty pounds of powder were used, the glass windows in the pilot house of the "Miantonomah" were shattered, and the captain and pilot driven down on deck. The procession up to the wharves was the greatest naval pageant ever seen in these waters, and one never to be forgotten by those who witnessed it. Thousands of people crowded the wharves, and lined the streets through which the funeral cortege passed on its way to City Hall, where the body of the great philanthropist was to lie in state. It was one of those beautiful days, sometimes seen in a New England winter, when everything is encased in armor of frost. The rigging of the ships in the harbor was covered with ice, the twigs of the trees were coated with it; and as the sun struck upon them the spectacle was one beautiful to look upon. The city and the ships seemed sheathed in glass.

ANOTHER GREAT NAVAL PAGEANT.—This was not the only great naval pageant in which I participated. I had the pleasure, in 1860, of piloting the British warship "Hero" into Portland Harbor, when that vessel came for the purpose of carrying back the Prince of Wales, who was just finishing his visit to these shores; and I also took in the battleship "Nile," sent from Halifax to act as the "Hero's" escort. When the Prince went on board and the yard-arms were manned, it was a pretty sight to see. He stood on the pilot bridge, going down the harbor, with the Duke of Newcastle by his side. The Duke's head-gear was novel to Western eyes, and the irreverent spectators raised a shout of "Oh, what a hat!"

But however the hat looked, the manning of the yard-arms was as handsome a sight as I ever saw. The sailors sprang to their places in a moment, at the word of command, and remained there as still as statues while the ceremony was going on. The spectacle was witnessed by a great crowd of people, for the city was thronged during the Prince's brief visit. Many of our old citizens, then young, will remember the occasion and the gala appearance Portland presented.

CHAPTER XVI.

I BECOME AN INVENTOR, AND PATENT A LIFE-PRESERVER. ANOTHER FRUITLESS SEARCH FOR THE SEA SERPENT.—A FUNNY FOURTH OF JULY IN PORTLAND.—HOW THE HAND ORGANS PLAYED IN LINCOLN PARK.—AN EARNEST PLEA FOR LIGHT HOUSE IMPROVEMENT.

AFTER having several close calls from being drowned I began to reflect that "self-preservation is the first law of nature," and so invented a rubber life-preserver, of which the accompanying cut conveys a good idea, and had it patented. It has been pronounced the neatest and most convenient article of the kind ever found of practical use. Its advantages over the ordinary belt life-preserver lie in the peculiarity of construction, which retains the flat, belt-like shape when inflated, its exceeding lightness, and its compactness. In the diagram the sectional view shows the walls, which keep it in form; the partitions being perforated so as to allow the air to pass freely to all parts.

It is so compact that it can be worn under the clothing, either about the waist or under the arms, without discovery, being secured in position by tapes as shown in the diagram. The inflating tube is flexible, and when the time for use arrives can be inflated in an instant; the wearer thus being prepared at once for the emergency. It has been found of especial benefit to bathers, as its size and form when inflated are such as not to impede the motions of the swimmer, and in cases of cramp has rendered inestimable service. I had it made in six sizes, from thirty-two to forty-four

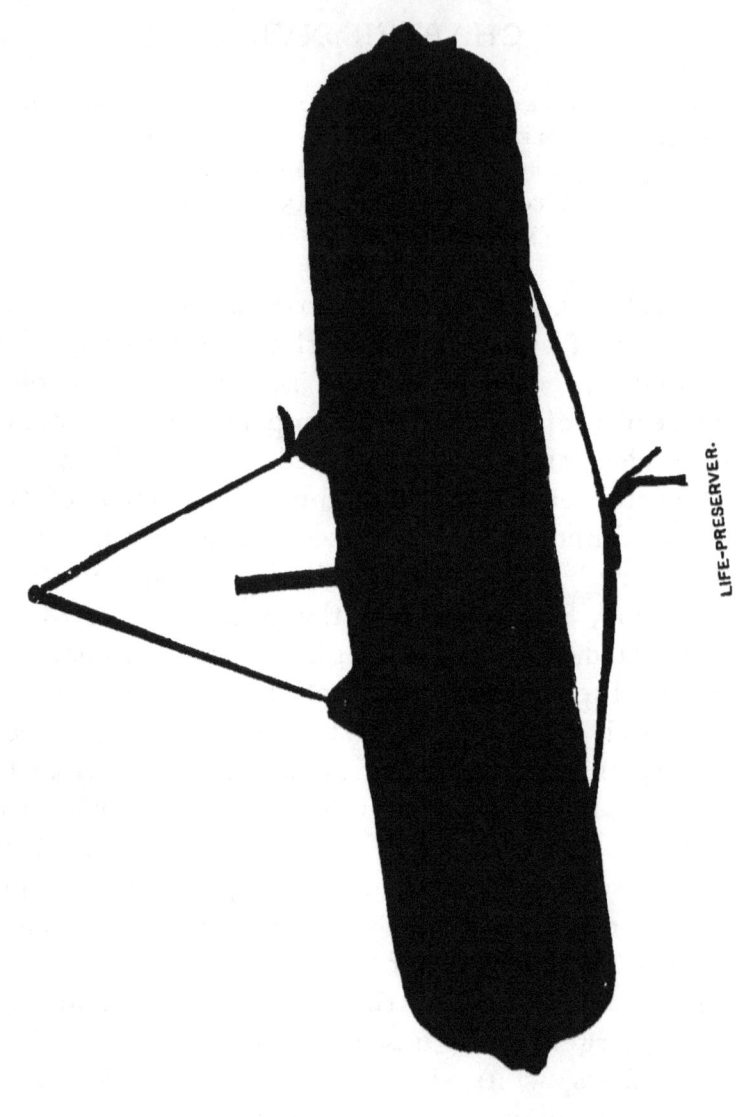

LIFE-PRESERVER.

inches in length, each when inflated being only two inches thick; and it proved very popular with seafaring men and all whom business or pleasure leads upon the water.

The summer of 1871 the pilot boat was used for fishing and sailing parties to the islands, and longer cruises along the coast. That fall I took the Richards brothers, who came down river from Richmond in a cat-boat, on a gunning excursion which lasted ten days. We had good sport and secured lots of game. The summer of 1872 was also good for fishing, and the luck was satisfactory. The sea serpent was reported off the coast this year, and I cruised two days for him, but failed to catch a glimpse of the monster.

My Cruise for the Sea Serpent.—In the summer of 1873, if I remember rightly, the sea serpent was again reported, off Boon Island this time. As my boat was receiving new rigging, I called on Captain Paul, of the yacht "Viva," to see if he would go out. He could not, but gave me the use of his yacht to cruise as long as I pleased. I got the following crew: K. D. Atwood, Alex Taylor, Theophilus Hopkins, E. Smith, and one or two others, with Mr. George O. Gosse as passenger. We cruised between Wood Island and Boon Island the first day, anchoring at Wood Island that night. The next morning we got under way, cruising broad off shore and to the eastward. When off Seguin we learned that the serpent had been seen the day before. We cruised as far east as Monhegan Island, and not seeing anything came home. The same day that we started for home, as we learned afterwards, the serpent was seen about eight or ten miles to the eastward of us. He was seen by two or three captains of fishing vessels. They were in sight of him some two or three hours, and one of the schooners started in search, but the wind being light could not gain on him. All who saw him give the same description of his head and neck, and say that he was going about four miles an hour, but as to the body and length they vary. They agree that he was only seen on calm, hot days.

I was well prepared with all kinds of implements and four hundred fathoms of line, and I had my mind made up not to harpoon him until near enough to the head to strike him between the eyes and destroy his sight at first stroke, and take my chances to back off from the lashing of his tail. When clear of the tail, I would give him all of the line by putting half barrels on each one-hundred-fathom section. Then I could watch his movements from the first half barrel and wait and let the iron do the killing. But the chance to test this plan never came. This season the serpent came on the coast with the herring and went east into the Bay of Fundy, in which he was seen several times during the summer. He went off the coast when the herring went. The last time he was reported was by one of our New York steamers when within about thirty miles of Cape Cod. It is my opinion that his native home is deep in the ocean and that he only comes up after food, near the surface, and perhaps at long intervals. If not a real sea serpent he has a head and neck resembling one, and is certainly a strange monster of the deep.

Though a great many disbelieve in the existence of the sea serpent there are numerous and well-authenticated instances in which he has been seen. No longer ago than 1833 five officers of the British army sailed in a yacht on a fishing excursion out of Halifax, Nova

Scotia. They got out farther to sea than they wished, and were returning in the afternoon when their attention was called to leeward by an exclamation of the old sailor who was acting as steersman of the boat. Looking to leeward they beheld, according to their sworn testimony sent to the *London Zoologist*, "at the distance of one hundred and fifty to two hundred yards, on our starboard bow, the head and neck of some denizen of the deep, precisely like those of a common snake, in the act of swimming, the head so far elevated and thrown forward by the curve of the neck as to enable us to see the water under and beyond it. The creature rapidly passed, leaving a regular wake, from the commencement of which to the forepart, which was out of the water, we judged its length to be about eighty feet, and this is within rather than beyond the mark. It is most difficult to give correctly the dimensions of any object in the water; but the head of the creature appeared to be about six feet in length, and the portion of the neck we saw the same. In thickness the neck equaled the trunk of a moderate-sized tree. The head and neck were of a dark brown or nearly black color, streaked with white in irregular streaks."

HOW THE HAND-ORGANS PLAYED IN LINCOLN PARK.—In the summer of 1873 our city government held some stormy meetings concerning a celebration on the Fourth of July, but failed to raise any money. We boys, young and old, were not satisfied with simply ringing of bells, so several of us "chipped in" to have some fun and a good celebration at not much expense. We sent a telegram to Boston to Mr. W. T. Brown, to see for what price he could get twenty hand-organs to come to Portland and play all day. The price given was five dollars each and expenses. We sent for them to be here in the morning on the Boston boat. I called on Mayor Wescott, and got a permit to put the bands in Lincoln Park. He said that Chandler's Band was engaged to give a concert in the evening. I promised him we would take our bands off the park by six o'clock in the afternoon and send them back to Boston by the seven o'clock boat. I left him laughing.

The evening and morning papers had notices that twenty bands were coming from Boston on the steamer to play in Lincoln Park, and that the best German and Italian music might be expected. On the arrival of the hand-organs here they were escorted from the boat to Mr. Bibber's, on India Street. At seven o'clock in the morning they were escorted to the park with orders to receive no money from the public on penalty of being discharged. On arrival at the park they were placed side by side, and the tunes permitted to mix. Eight of them were placed around the fountain and the others at the different walks coming into the park. There they stood five hours in the forenoon and five in the afternoon, not saying a word to any one and playing away for dear life. I have never seen so many people in the park since it was opened. It was crowded all day, as there was no other spot in the whole city to see any fun. Everybody I met felt pleased with the music and the crowd went off the park shouting with laughter. The bands were paid off at Bibber's, highly pleased with their pay and treatment and wishing to come again.

I am in favor of a fair celebration on the Fourth of July. It brings lots of money into the city and some, even many, get a benefit in all kinds of trade. Our citizens here are paying taxes to run the city government, and our city fathers should do something to celebrate one day in the year at least. If they want a cheap celebration, I advise them to send to Boston and get an army of hand-organs at five dollars apiece and expenses. Many teams were on this occasion offered us free to take the organs and march around town, more particularly to serenade those gentlemen that voted against a celebration.

OUR LIGHT-HOUSES. — In the course of these recollections considerable has been said of our light-houses, and further facts concerning those most familiar may be of interest. The building of Portland Head Light-house began in 1788, and it was finished and first lighted January 10, 1791.

The building of Half Way Rock Light-house began in 1869, and it was first lighted August 15, 1871. This light is very valuable to masters and pilots coming into Portland from the east, and no doubt has saved many lives and a large amount of property. By its aid vessels get into port or shelter from strong gales, when otherwise they would have to haul off from the coast and take the consequences. Many coasters, perhaps most, are not prepared to meet bad gales.

The light-house board made a bad mistake in 1855, when the western Cape Light was discontinued. Captains on long voyages and unaware of the change would, on reaching the coast by night and seeing but one light, invariably keep off if the wind were fair, and go to Seguin. There, too, they would find but one light, and in consequence would be completely puzzled as to their position. Several vessels came near being wrecked by the change. In 1856 the pilots and masters petitioned Congress for a return of the old method of lighting, and the change back to two lights was made.

Portland Head Light has been cut down twenty feet (I think twice, the last time in 1883) and the power reduced from second order to fourth order lens. It could not be seen far in even clear weather. Mr. Robinson's house near Pond Cove used to have a lamp at the window which was as bright as that at the Head. Probably they used dogfish oil. After continual protest by pilots and masters a reef was shook out and hoisted up twenty feet and the second power lens put back. There has been no change since, and I hope there never will be again, as the light is satisfactory to all mariners. While I was in the pilot boat "Nettle" I had a good chance to see the lights, and cheerfully give all the light-house keepers credit for keeping the lights in first-class order. I don't cruise outside nowadays, but think of those who do. People who stay at home and live in rooms kept at seventy to seventy-five degrees of heat don't know much about the weather outside, or the hardships on the water in the cold winters.

AN EARNEST PLEA FOR THE FOG-BELL. — Masters and pilots need a good bell on the Breakwater, but some of our light-house inspectors are opposed to it. A strong petition has been offered and ignored. It should be heeded. Portland Harbor will never be as it should be until a decent bell that can be heard is put up and a light at Spring Point. I may not need it, but those who follow me will. No less than two and a half million people pass in and out of this harbor yearly, and a great amount of property is carried to and fro. Big ocean carriers in winter, passenger and pleasure boats in summer, costly yachts from New York and all along the coast, ply our waters. It is criminal to put all this to risk. I am surprised that any government officer sent to observe this coast and its harbors should think a proper bell dangerous or misleading, and as long as I live shall never cease to work for it. When I am gone I hope my friends will keep the good work up until our masters and pilots have what they and the public need for the protection of life and property.

The bell buoy put near the Breakwater by the government in 1893 is entirely useless for its destined purpose, though it might do well enough as a roost for the swans that swim in the little pond in Deering's Oaks. Side-wheel steamers, after passing the buoy, sometimes ring the bell by the motion of their wheels in the water; but propellers and sailing vessels would have to run into it to make it sound.

I am glad to learn that the government is about to place a bell on Stanford Ledge to be rung by electricity. It has been needed for years, and steamboat captains and pilots will rejoice. When a light and bell have been placed on Spring Point Ledge they will rejoice still more, and feel safe in entering our harbor in any weather, no matter how thick.

CHAPTER XVII.

DAYS WHEN A HOGSHEAD OF COAL LASTED PORTLAND A WHOLE SEASON.—MR. SAMUEL E. SPRING AND THE GOVERNMENT SALE OF CIGARS.—GUNNING ON RICHMOND ISLAND.—FORMATION OF THE WILLARD SHOOTING ASSOCIATION.—PAT AND THE LOON.

DURING all these years the stevedoring business in Portland had increased, steam-hoisting engines largely taking the place of horses. The coal trade steadily developed, until it has now reached unexpected proportions. It was about 1826, I am told, that Capt. John Waite brought the first hard coal to Portland from Philadelphia in a hogshead lashed on his quarter-deck. He brought, too, an open-grate stove to burn it in; and when he started the fire all the neighbors flocked to his house to see him burn "the rocks," as they called them. The next year he brought sixty tons and several more stoves. When I began stevedoring, in 1853, about 11,000 tons were brought to this port. In 1894 the total number was 653,000, and the demand is constantly increasing.

A CURIOUS TRANSACTION IN CIGARS.—But coal was not the only commodity I handled. Many years ago the government sold over 200,000 cigars, stored in a warehouse on Atlantic Wharf. The day before the sale people had the privilege of sampling them, and Mr. Samuel E. Spring called on me to go down with him. On going through the cigars we came across one lot of 40,000, with a rough wrapper on them, and on cutting the cigars open found long fillers and splendid tobacco. The most of them were fancy brands with smooth and handsome wrappers, but filled with poor tobacco. This lot was an exception. Mr. Spring said to me if he bought any I could have them at cost. The fancy brands were sold first. The bidder was to take nothing less than 5,000, but more if he so wished. When the 40,000 were sold there was slow bidding; those present supposing that Mr. Spring, who made a bid, only wanted a small lot for his own use.

The cigars were sold to Mr. Spring, and when asked how many he wanted he said he would take the lot, and asked me how many I would take. I told him 5,000. A few days later my friend, Doctor Gale, wanted 200 or 300 to try the brand, and I sold them to him. Shortly after a Custom House officer called on me and asked me if I sold some cigars to Doctor Gale. I told him that I did. He said that he should have to impose a fine on me for selling cigars without the government stamp. I told him that I did not know that I was liable, as I bought them for my own use and was not in the habit of selling cigars, but let the doctor have those to try. I asked him if he was joking or in earnest. He said he was in earnest, and was quite stiff about it. I told him the cigars were bought by Mr. S. E. Spring at government auction at Atlantic Wharf some days before. He asked, "Are these the cigars?" I told him they were, and that was the last that I heard about the matter.

Sometime in the seventies Collector Washburn thought I was a smuggler, and put me under one thousand dollar bonds, Mr. William Senter becoming my bondsman. I was much surprised at the charge, but discovered subsequently that it was made to divert the attention of the real offenders and give the officers a chance to pounce upon them.

GUNNING AND GAME ON RICHMOND'S ISLAND.— In the spring of 1879 we gunners chartered the sloop "Rocky Mountain," Capt. Ben Hamilton, to go for a shooting trip. We were all day getting to Richmond's Island. Game was plentiful and we had fine sport. Mr. J. F. Randall and Capt. Ben Hamilton in one boat, Joseph F. Fowler and myself in the other, went near the Kirkwood House and had our decoys all set before daylight. As soon as daylight the game came plenty and over the decoys, near enough to see their eyes. Fowler would shoot on his side of the boat, and I on mine. He would let go two barrels and I the same. I would ask, "What you got, Fowler?" He would say, "Nothing, what you got?" "Nothing," would be my reply. The fact was we could not shoot well on the wing, but we had a good chance to practice and kept at it. Sometimes a large flock would come near and we would give them four barrels, bring down five or six, and get them. They were so thick that the shot would take them three or four feet from where we pointed. So we were shooting behind them. When one would light at the decoys we had him. We used muzzle-loaders, but this time I had Mr. George Round's breech-loader. The game would come right back again before we could load the muzzle-loaders, and by having the two guns I got mixed up a little. As my gun was half loaded when the game came I would pick up the breech-loader and fire. Finally I got two charges of shot in one barrel and two of powder in the other. When game came one barrel would not kill and the other would not go off. Then Fowler had the laugh on me. At noon, when our ammunition gave out, we had about twenty birds, mostly of the coot species. We went on board to dinner, got a new supply of ammunition, went back, and set the decoys. The game came as flush as ever. I left the breech-loader on board as the cartridges gave out, and used the muzzle-loader. We had better luck in the afternoon until I lost my ramrod while ramming the wad down. The air sent it some fifteen feet overboard. So after that Fowler would shoot and I would pick them up. I really think if we had been good for shooting on the wing with breech-loaders, we could have got a boat full. During the day we got thirty-eight game, and thought we did well, as our boat was high line. I think if Randall and Hamilton had had our places they could have got a hundred. We all had great sport and good weather. The party in three days got some over two hundred game.

THE ADVANTAGES OF POSSESSING A BAROMETER. —May 17, 1880, the yacht "T. B. Davis" was chartered with Capt. Nat Haskell for a shooting trip, and carried the following party: J. F. Randall, Joseph F. Fowler, George Stanwood, Ben Hamilton, Taylor, and myself. We had good sport. Late one afternoon we anchored at Stratton Island. The wind was southwest with not a cloud to be seen. After supper Mr. Randall and some of the party went on shore to get milk and eggs. Soon after they left I looked at the barometer and saw it was falling fast and a gale near at hand. Presently the boat came off. At this time it was calm. I told them to hoist the boats on deck. We would hoist in two and tow one. Several said it would be a good night to lay there; but I told them it was no harbor for a north wind, and the anchor would not hold her off the rocks. The first whiff of wind we got under way to go to Richmond's Harbor. Before we got a mile from Stratton Island the wind came with a rush and we had to shorten sail at once. It was a cold north wind, and when we anchored at Richmond's Harbor it took both anchors to hold her. The wind was a gale with plenty of white caps on the water. The next day was good for gunning and game. We gunned in the forenoon and came home in the afternoon with all the game we wanted; and when we arrived home, all that wanted a pair of birds had them free. It was fun to see the game go up Commercial Street. Everybody knew that the gunners had got home.

This shows the advantage of a barometer. I got one in 1859, when I bought the pilot boat "Nettle," have made a close study of it ever since, and still keep it. The farmers should have one to tell them when to cut the grass. Oftentimes they cut it on a high glass because it is clear and hot weather. Then come east winds and fog, and the grass turns black before they get sun to make it. Should the sun come out at noon for a short time it heats the grass, which is bad for the hay.

May 7, 1881, the fishing schooner "Agnes Bell" was chartered by our gunning party for a fourteen days' cruise to the eastward. We wanted to go to Point La Prow for brant shooting, but were baffled. We had the wind east and raining most of the time, and the barometer was high all of the trip. G. F. Loveitt and myself thought we would open the barometer to see if we could get better weather. On turning a screw on the back she went down to typhoon mark; so we turned back the screw and let her rest. We got as far east as Crumple Island and went ashore to see the Portland gunning party which was there. Mr. Martin, who was of the party, treated me to a pop cocktail. I can't say what the others took. I give this party credit for saving lives from wrecks in a gale,

J. N. MARTIN, PRESIDENT OF THE WILLARD SHOOTING ASSOCIATION.

when on one of these cruises, by going to an island inside, breaking in the door of the life-saving boathouse, getting the life-boat out, and saving the crews. The life savers were off pay until fall, and so no one was at the station. After that government bought part of Crumple Island, as it was an outside island.

During our trip east we only captured one hundred and thirty sea game. On the way home we saw lots of game, but it was too rough and rainy to go in small boats for them.

THE WILLARD SHOOTING ASSOCIATION.—January 27, 1881, the Willard Shooting Association was organized with Mr. J. N. Martin, President, and Capt. B. J. Willard, Vice-President. The association leased land of Ami Whitney, in Falmouth Foreside, and put up a club-house that cost $250. After the house was built and ready we had fine sport shooting glass balls from the trap for practice. We invited other clubs from the state and had good, friendly shoots on our grounds. During 1882 we returned their visits.

April 19, 1883, we had a very interesting match game at the club grounds at Falmouth with the Riverside Club of Topsham, Me. The match was very close and the score as follows:

WILLARD SHOOTING ASSOCIATION.

	Single pigeons, 20.	Double pigeons, 8.	Glass balls, 20.	Total, 40 birds.
Randall,	17	19	Total,	36
Willard,	20	17	"	37
Harmon,	19	17	"	36
Todd,	16	15	"	31
McKenney,	15	15	"	30
Davis,	17	16	"	33
Martin,	15	17	"	32
Noyes,	15	16	"	31

F. Merrill,		15	17	Total, 32
Deane, .		13	16	" 29
Hawkins,		16	17	" 33
Hall, . .		13	13	" 26
Day, . .		14	19	" 33
		205	214	419

RIVERSIDE CLUB.

Single pigeons, 20.   Double pigeons, 8.   Glass balls, 20.   Total, 40 birds.

C. L. York, .		14	14	Total, 28
A. L. Goud, .	.	15	18	" 33
C. Goud, .		15	17	" 32
G. Goud, .		18	14	" 32
A. Hall, .		16	16	" 32
Mc. Hall, .		19	17	" 36
C. Winslow, .		15	15	" 30
A. Perry, .		16	16	" 32
C. Hayes,		20	16	" 36
S. Knight,		14	18	" 32
H. Stetson, .		15	15	" 30
G. E. Keene,		12	11	" 23
S. Strout, .	.	15	16	" 31
		204	203	407

PAT AND THE BIG DUCK.—May 5, 1882, we gunners chartered the pilot boat "Maggie," Captain Poor, to go shooting between Richmond Island and Wood Island. The party consisted of J. F. Randall, J. F. Fowler, Mr. Farrington, and myself. Randall and Fowler went in one boat, G. F. Loveitt and myself in another; Farrington with Captain Poor. We had the best fun shooting that we had seen for a long time. Loveitt and myself bagged fifty-two sea game in two and one-half hours at what is called "Old Proprietor." The game came so fast our guns got hot, so they were uncomfortable to handle. After shooting four days we returned home, having three hundred and thirteen birds total, ninety-six of which were old squaws. When we were at the wharf all parties coming for birds were given a pair, and the birds were flying all over the city. I saw a man on the wharf by the name of Pat and asked him if he did not want a mess of birds. He said he did, and I told him to come down the ladder and get them. I gave him two, and Pat asked me what I was going to do with that big duck. I told him he could have him if he wished. The big duck was a monstrous big loon, nearly three feet long. When Pat got on the wharf he took the pair of birds in one hand and the loon by the legs in the other, its head dragging on the ground. I never learned how Pat got the feathers off from him.

CHAPTER XVIII.

HOW THE "BROOKLYN" STRUCK ON HOG ISLAND LEDGE.—OLD NEPTUNE VISITS THE PILOT BOAT "MAGGIE" AND SHAVES THE PASSENGERS.—MR. STROUT'S ENCOUNTER WITH A SWORD FISH. SOMETHING ABOUT SPANISH MACKEREL.

ABOUT eleven o'clock the night of April 6, 1883, the steamship "Brooklyn" of the Dominion Line steamed out to sea on her way across the Atlantic—a trip she was not destined to complete that time trying. Being the stevedore for the line, I was on the wharf with Captain Reed and Messrs. Torrance and Scanlan to see the ship off, and then went home.

About midnight my door bell rang violently, and on answering it I found Mr. Dufriends, who said that the "Brooklyn" was in trouble down the harbor and sending up rockets. He wanted to get a tug boat to go to her relief. Mr. Torrance soon after drove up in a hack, and we went to Capt. A. S. Oliver to engage the tow-boat "Express." As soon as steam was up we started. Our supposition was that the "Brooklyn" had run into some vessel, and then anchored; but we found her ashore on the southwest point of Hog Island Ledge. Returning to the city, we took a team to look up lighters to go down in the morning as soon as possible to lighten the cargo. We tried to get Captain Hamilton's sloop, the "M. M. Hamilton," but she was being stripped to receive a gang of rigging. So we went to Knightville, to the house of another Captain Hamilton, and secured all the lighters we wanted, five or six in number. The cargo was promptly discharged,

CAPTAIN WILLARD AS NEPTUNE.

landed at the Grand Trunk sheds, and later sold at auction. The Boston steamer was obtained from Mr. Coyle to take out the live stock. The work went on night and day, and gave employment to a large number of men. At the same time I had two ships at the wharf, making the largest pay-roll I ever had in one week since going into the stevedoring business. I had Mr. Albert B. Hall with me to assist in paying off the laborers. The "Brooklyn" was discharged, floated, and put into the dry dock, where temporary repairs were made to enable her to cross the ocean.

AN INTERVIEW WITH OLD NEPTUNE. — May 11, 1883, a party consisting of J. F. Randall, Doctor Cummings, Doctor Merrill, Dr. George Fyre, J. F. Fowler, G. F. Loveitt, H. Trefethen, and myself went on a six days' shooting trip in the pilot boat "Maggie," Captain Parsons. We found sport good and bagged four hundred and sixty-six sea game, the birds being given away to those who wished for them when we got home.

Our next trip gunning in the "Maggie" was with about the same party. I found that the most of our sailors had never crossed the equator, so thought I would have some fun. I called at Littlefield's and got a suit to dress up as Neptune; a mask, long, gray beard, wig to match, a comical hat, and a suit to go with it. This was put on board the boat in charge of the cook, who was enjoined not to let the party know anything about it. I called on Lyman, Son & Tobey for a speaking trumpet, and Mr. Guptill made me a present of one. I had a nice razor for the occasion, one that I captured at a whist party as a booby prize. I let Mr. Loveitt into the secret, and told him when Neptune hailed the ship "Maggie" to call all the sailors on deck. Wood Island Pool was to answer for the

PILOT BOAT "MAGGIE," CAPT. EDWARD L. PARSONS.

equator. So one morning after breakfast, while the party in the cabin were having a smoke, I went on deck to the forecastle and told the cook to pass up my box. I dressed up as Neptune. When ready I hailed the ship "Maggie." Loveitt came out of the gangway and called all hands on deck. When on deck I informed them that all sailors who had never crossed the equator before would be shaved by Neptune. When the razor was taken out of the case it was found to be nearly two feet in length. As I advanced aft to perform the shaving Doctor Merrill was frightened and started to jump overboard. Mr. Randall caught him by the coat and I advanced and gave a dry shave. The usual custom is to use strong-smelling slush for lather. I looked around for Doctor Frye and he had slunk into the cabin. I sent the quartermaster after him and he brought him up. About the time I got through shaving the sailors, Mr. Hussey, of Wood Island Pool, rowed off with some clams for the party. When he got sight of Neptune he started to row away. Neptune told him to come back for he would not hurt him. Mr. Hussey said that he had read a good deal about Neptune, but never saw him before.

LONG HOURS AND SWEET SLEEP.—I would give the morning call at 1 A. M., for the gunners to turn out, breakfast at 1.30, and start away in their gunning boats at 2 with lunch and coffee to get on the gunning ground and have the decoy set by daylight, so as to be ready to shoot when the game came. Each boat would try to get ahead of the other in bagging game. Usually we got back to the pilot boat about 4 P. M., and counted the game. Then it was clean up the guns and get ready for the next day, and then have supper. By this time the party would be pretty tired, so all slept well.

We had one good rule and kept it strictly, and that was that no gunner should pass his gun from the pilot boat to his boat loaded, or from small boat to pilot boat loaded. The penalty for violation of this rule was a dollar fine. By this means we never had any accidents by shooting. When two men were in the boat the man forward would keep the muzzle of his gun pointing forward, and the man aft, the muzzle of his pointed aft; so if a gun should be accidentally discharged nobody would get hurt. I believe Mr. Fowler once shot a dory bird, and Mr. Randall a boat bird. On this trip the total number of birds bagged was three hundred and seventy-two, mostly old squaws. There were only sixteen coots in the lot.

May 7, 1887, the party was smaller and we gunned two days, getting one hundred and eleven birds. May 10, 1888, was the last gunning trip I made in the "Maggie," when we got two hundred and eighty-eight birds.

SWORD–FISHING BY STEAM.—In the summer of 1883 I built a steam water boat, called the "Fannie G.," to tow and fill water in my hoisting scows, and September 2, 1884, made my first sword-fish trip in her with Capt. D. Peterson and the following party: Hon. A. A. Strout, Mr. John B. Curtis, John Bacon, of Illinois, William Taylor, A. H. Mantine, T. E. Sumner, of New York, and H. T. Strout. We left Portland at eight o'clock in the morning.

Sword-fish was reported off Cape Porpoise. When off Boon Island we saw one, but could not get near him. In the afternoon the wind breezed up, and it was some choppy. We harbored at Portsmouth and the party stopped at a hotel. We took in coal and water for the next day. At two o'clock in the morning we started down river, steamed off to the south of the Isle of Shoals, among several vessels looking for sword-fish, and steamed to the northeast. About ten o'clock we sighted a fish, harpooned him, and soon had him on board. About eleven, in running down towards Boon Island, I saw another under water and had just time to harpoon him. The boat was stopped and backed. We hauled him along-side, put gaffs in him, and pulled him on board. He lay still, and I got another iron ready and got out to the pulpit to look for more. As the party gathered around the fish he all at once began to jump, and I thought that he would jump overboard. In jumping he knocked Mr. Curtis, Mr. Strout, and one other man down on deck. I got in as soon as possible, took a club and hit him on his sword, which stilled him. It was fun to see the party run aft. I had to laugh heartily. Some minutes later Mr. Strout said, "Ben, I believe you did that on purpose."

Later we saw one more, but could not get on him, as all the fish were shy at sight of so many vessels after them. By this time it was getting late in the afternoon and we had a long way to go to Portland. When near Boon Island Ledge I told the party that this ledge was famous for rock cod in summer, so they wished to try it. We had good bait on ice. We hove to, and as soon as the lines went down to the bottom there was a good-sized cod-fish on the hook. Not having any tub to put them into, they were put on the deck until it was covered half-knee deep. The party enjoyed the sport hugely. I had hard work to get Curtis and Strout to start for home. I think that they would have kept on fishing until dark. We finally got started. During the two days water and weather were all that could be asked for, and the trip will long be remembered by all on board. The party arrived at Portland near eight o'clock in the evening. The next morning the sword-fish were landed. One weighed about five hundred pounds, and the smallest one two hundred and seventy-seven pounds. The cod was given to friends. Most of the party never saw large fish captured before, and some were never on salt water until this trip, so you see it was a great sight for them. A trip like this is good for a business man, allowing him to escape from business cares, and he never forgets it.

FEEDING GROUNDS OF SWORD-FISH.—I have been asked to give the different feeding grounds for sword-fish. They are known to be plenty off the southeast coast of Japan. Some are found to the north of New Zealand. They are also seen to the west of Mexico and from Newfoundland along the east coast of North and South America to the river La Plata. They are again found from Norway on the west coast of Europe, and south around Africa up the east coast to the Red Sea. A few are on the west coast of Ceylon, a few in the China Sea, and in the South Atlantic along twenty degrees west and twenty south latitude. As a centre they appear to spread over a surface of six hundred miles square. This is about half way from the Isle of St. Helena to the coast of South America.

SPANISH MACKEREL.—As to Spanish mackerel we find the following in the "Fisherman's Memorial and Record Book," which gives an idea of the abundance of the species in Massachusetts Bay in the early part of the present century: "In 1812 a large school of Spanish mackerel visited this bay; and so plenty and numerous were they that they would bite readily at the bare hooks, and seize upon small bits of line hanging

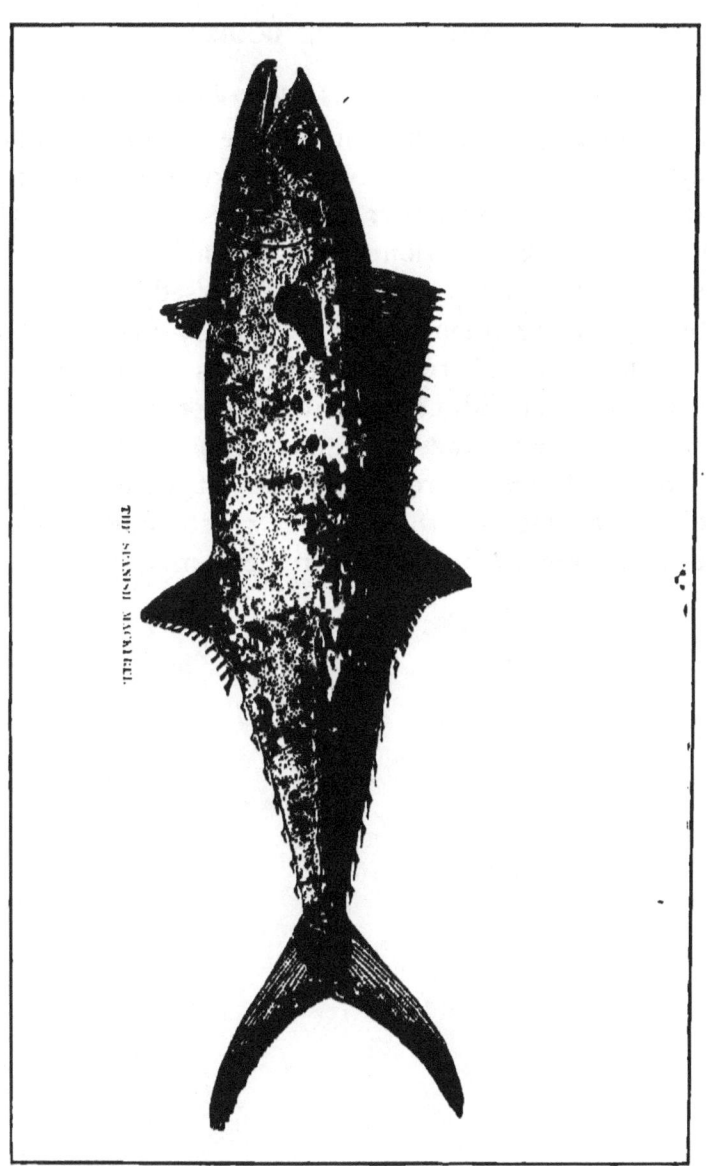

THE SPANISH MACKEREL.

from the vessel. Standing-room boats were then mostly in use, holding from fifteen to twenty tons. These rooms held from fifteen to twenty barrels and the crews would catch them full in a few hours. Mr. Timothy, at Rowe's Bank, at Gloucester, Mass., bought most of these mackerel fresh, after being dressed, at two cents a pound, salting them in his building; and the business, which lasted two months, was a lively one." These mackerel did not continue on this coast more than a few years and have now almost entirely disappeared. There were a few caught with the other mackerel as late as 1825, since which time it is very rare to see one during the entire season.

CHAPTER XIX.

THE SCHOONER "B. J. WILLARD" AND HER FORTUNES. HOW STEAMERS HAVE TAKEN THE FREIGHTS FROM SAILING VESSELS. —THE WAY IN WHICH I CELEBRATED THE PORTLAND CENTENNIAL.—ABOUT THE WATER BOAT "FANNIE G." — SUNFISH AND THEIR CURIOUS FORMATION.

THE schooner "B. J. Willard" was contracted for by my brother Charles, who was lost at sea about a month after making his contract, while on his way from Philadelphia to Portland in his schooner "Georgie Deering." He was overtaken by a heavy gale from the northeast in the vicinity of Cape Cod, on the 9th of March, 1872, and no tidings of the crew or vessel have come from that day to this.

My nephew, B. F. Woodbury, soon after took charge of building and fitting her for sea, and went master. She sailed from Bath, Me., with a cargo of ice for Philadelphia, September 20, 1872, on her first voyage. The last of November, 1876, we sold her to Bolton, Bliss & Dallett, for a packet to run between New York and Venezuelan ports. In about two years' time the firm were compelled to put on a line of steamers or lose their business. The "Willard," with the rest of the sailing vessels, was sold. In 1879 she became a total wreck upon a reef near a salt port in the Mediterranean. While we owned her she ran with few mishaps.

It may be of interest to some of my friends to read her record. She was one of the first three-masted schooners built and owned in Portland. At the time

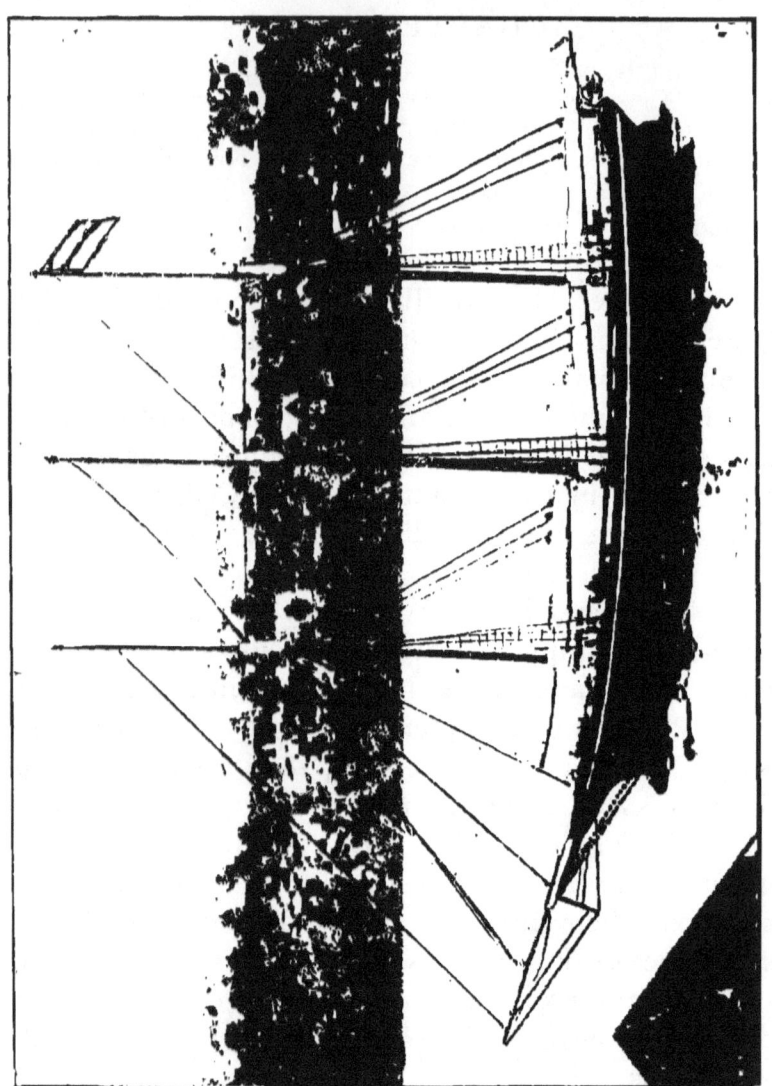

THE SCHOONER "B. J. WILLARD."

she was building, the Bath ship-owners looked upon three-masted schooners in disgust, although their builders were building, that year, quite a fleet of this class of vessels for Cape Cod, Taunton, and New Jersey captains, on contract. It did not take the ship-owners long to see there was more money in this class of vessels than in their larger wooden ships which had to come in competition with English iron ships which were given a preference of five shillings per ton freight, besides favor given by English Lloyds insurance companies. The "Willard" was built to carry 500 tons of coal. At that time this size of vessel was considered a large vessel, and we were bothered to get that much cargo very often. She was built to run as a packet between Portland and Philadelphia. There was a nice business in out freights of mackerel, herring, oil carpeting, shovel handles, canned corn, and sundry other goods; freights back to Portland, on coal, varying from $2 to $4 per ton, according to the season. Sugar freights, at that time, from the north side of Cuba were from $5 to $7 a hogshead. Times have changed now; all the general freight going from Portland to Philadelphia is being shipped by the way of the New York steamers or Boston boats and forwarded by steamers to its destination. As the manufacturing plants increase the coal orders enlarge, and at this time it is more common to have a cargo of coal arrive here of 2,000 tons than it was of 500 in 1872. The "Willard" was noted for her good sailing qualities; and the first two years for the good dividends to her owners. I will give here a statement of her earnings as made up from her books by Capt. B. F. Woodbury:

Sailing from Bath September 18, 1872, her first dividend was declared October 16th, and amounted to

$694.92; her second, of $700, December 4th; her third, $879.54, on March 3, 1873; fourth, $1,600, May 5th; fifth, $1,280, June 13th; sixth, $2,400, September 18th; seventh, $647.60, October 11th — a total of $8,157.06.

All bills for her construction and outfit were paid September 14, 1872, her cost being $23,985.82.

The last dividend was paid November 30, 1876, and brought the total up to $20,525.22. She was then sold for $18,752.96, thus bringing to her owners, above cost, $15,292.36.

The cost of running the vessel for the four years and two months was $6,970.94. The total amount of freights earned was $76,605.94.

In January, 1874, she went from Portland to Matanzas with freight which earned $1,195.11, and thence to Philadelphia with molasses at $4 a hogshead, which brought $3,662.92; a total for the round trip of $4,858.03. This was made inside of two months from leaving Portland.

How I Celebrated the Centennial.—July 4, 1886, Portland's centennial celebration occurred, and it was a grand affair. There were in the harbor at the time five warships, the "Yantic," "Swatara," "Tennessee," "Galena," and the French warship "Talisman." They were all trimmed with flags, as were the other vessels, and it was the grandest sight ever seen in Portland Harbor. The weather was perfect. At that time I was the harbor master, and I got an order to move the mud dredge out of the channel to give a clear course for a rowing regatta from Union Wharf to Fish Point and return. I got a boy in an express wagon to take me on Munjoy Hill to see Mr. Gerrish to have the dredge moved, which was promptly done by hauling it to the end of Franklin Wharf.

In coming down the hill on my return, and near the Portland Company office, the whiffletree dropped on the horse's heels and he ran away. The driver could not control him, and when near Mountfort Street everything looked wild. I balanced myself, jumped over the forward wheel, and landed on the ground; and when I struck it broke both bones of the left leg near the ankle and I rolled over against the fence of the Portland Company yard. My foot was numb, and I did not know the bones were broken until I started to get up. The first man I saw coming was Capt. Scott Oliver. He was soon followed by others, and I was taken home in a grocery wagon near at hand. It was a hard celebration for me, and one that I shall never forget.

My steamer "Fannie G." was engaged with a sloop lighter to visit the warships and get brass field-pieces with sailors to go in the procession. It was one of the finest parades ever in Portland.

WHY I LEFT OFF SMOKING CIGARS. — In the year 1888 I had a stroke of paralysis on the left side, caused by smoking cigars and getting my blood full of nicotine. While smoking I felt no ill effect and it never seemed to shake my nerves. I called Dr. H. P. Merrill. His advice was to stop smoking cigars, and that advice I have kept, and shall the rest of my life. He brought me out of it in a few days. At times my heart would beat hard, and I supposed that I had heart disease, as there were a great many dropping off with that trouble; but after I stopped smoking I never had any more trouble with my heart. Now I would advise my friends to take warning and not smoke too many cigars. Men with business on their minds will smoke a great many more cigars than they are aware of, and oftentimes they feel the bad effects when it is too late.

THE "FANNIE G." AND HER GOOD WORK.—The water boat, "Fannie G.," of which I have before spoken, proved excellent for her purpose, and did much good service, some in saving property as well as affording considerable pleasure to fishing parties. She was in pretty constant use, filling the light-house tanks at Half Way Rock and Seguin, serving warships in the harbor, and protecting the water front against fire. It might be tedious to give a detailed account of her work, but I will offer a specimen or two. February 6, 1890, she pumped sixteen and a half hours at the fire on Brown's Wharf, and at the same time saved the clubhouse on Merchants' Wharf; using the small number five Dean pump with which she had so often done valuable service. In November of that same year she played on the Richardson Wharf fire, pumping two hours through two lines of hose with one-inch nozzles of the new number eight Dean pump, and rendering great aid.

July 21, 1885, took a fishing party on the "Fannie G." We had luck and caught lots of good cod.

July 22d took another party to Cod Ledge with the usual good luck.

August 16th filled tank with water for one year's supply at Half Way Rock Light.

July 17, 1887, again filled the Half Way Rock Light, and also the two warships, "Richmond" and "Yantic."

August 6, 1888, again filled Half Way Rock Light.

September 4th took out a fishing party, had fine luck, and got from five to six hundred pounds of fish.

September 10th carried a lot of voters from Cundy's Harbor to Harpswell and back.

July 8, 1889, again filled the Half Way Rock

STEAM WATER BOAT, "FANNIE G.," CAPT. DANIEL PETERSON, 1883.

Light, and pumped salt water to Seguin Light-house through 600 feet of hose and 136 feet rise, on the west side of the island.

September 17th filled the Seguin Light-house tank with salt water, to run the whistle, through 1,800 feet of hose, from the harbor, 136 feet rise. This was done with a number five Dean pump, small size.

February 6, 1890, the "Fannie G." pumped sixteen and a half hours for the city, during the fire at Brown's Wharf, and at the same time saved the club-house at Merchants' Wharf, with this same small number five Dean pump.

June 28th pumped out the schooner "Mathew Kenney," at Cundy's Harbor, and towed her to Portland.

During July and August filled with water the United States warships "Kearsarge," "Petrel," and "Baltimore." At this time we had just put in the new large number eight Dean fire pump.

November 26th the "Fannie G." was called to the Richardson Wharf fire, and pumped two hours, through two lines of hose with one-inch nozzles of the new number eight, the Dean pump doing good service.

June 24, 1891, pumped out the schooner "O. P. Lord," at Birch Island Ledge, and towed her back to Portland.

June 30th pumped 10,000 gallons of fresh water and 20,000 gallons of salt water, through 3,300 feet of hose, with about 140 feet rise, into the tank of the Ottawa House, Cushing's Island. A number eight Dean pump was used. It was a great surprise to the boarders.

August 24th pumped out the yacht "Viking," at Falmouth Foreside; and also filled with water the United States warships "Chicago," "Atlanta," "Yorktown," "Boston," and "Concord."

July 20, 1892, pumped out the schooner "A. H. Robinson," at Small Point, and towed her to Portland.

September 27th pumped out the Grand Trunk Railroad pontoon.

August 31, 1893, pumped out the schooner "Julia Baker," at Cape Elizabeth.

November 18th pumped out the Portland Bridge pontoon.

December 12th pumped out the "P. J. Hession's" scow, at Cape Elizabeth.

August 23, 1894, went to Richmond Island, pumped out the "A. M. Dearing," and towed her to Portland in company with the tug "Demerrest," Capt. George Mathews.

December 17th pumped on the bark "V. M. Hopkins" some thirty-eight hours.

December 29th pumped out the pontoon at the Ferry Slip, Portland Pier.

THE PURSUIT OF THE SUNFISH.—In July, 1893, she went out with the following party for deep-sea fishing: F. D. Rogers, George Thayer, Capt. H. E. Willard, Edward Keene, F. H. Little, H. A. Clay, and myself. We first went on the eastern part of Rock Cod Ledge, and not finding the cod-fish very plenty started for the western shoal. In steaming up, some of the party saw a black fin sticking up, and the boat was turned for it at once. It proved to be a large sunfish. When near it I drove the harpoon at its head. The gristle in the head was so hard that the harpoon only entered about an inch, and as I put my weight on the staff the iron shank bent up. I could not get the harpoon in any deeper. The fish sank when the line came taut, and the iron came out and we supposed that we should not see him again; but to our surprise he

SUNFISH. 6 FEET 5 INCHES LONG, 5 FEET DEEP; WEIGHT ABOUT 600 POUNDS.

came to the surface. We turned around and steamed for him once more. This time I struck him well aft and the iron went half-way through him. After that we captured him easily, though it took all hands to haul him on deck. The rest of the day was spent in cod-fishing, on the western shoal of Cod Ledge, and we caught all the cod that we wanted. On returning home we tied a rope to the sunfish and left him at the Forest City Landing, Peaks Island, so the boarders and visitors could see him.

Several species of this odd-looking fish have been captured in British waters, and in almost every case the creature was swimming, or rather floating, in so lazy a fashion that it permitted itself to be taken without attempting to escape. In the seas where this fish is generally found, the harpoon is usually used for its capture; not so much on account of its strength, though a large specimen will sometimes struggle with amazing force and fury, but on account of its great weight, which renders its conveyance into a boat a matter of some little difficulty.

The flesh of the sunfish is white, well flavored, and in much request among sailors, who always luxuriate in fresh meat after the monotony of salted provisions. In flavor and aspect it somewhat resembles the skate. Its liver is rather large and yields a large amount of oil, which is prized by the sailors as an infallible remedy for sprains, burns, bruises, and rheumatic affections. One of its most curious peculiarities is the structure of the eyes, which are bedded in a mass of very soft and flexible folds belonging to the outer membranous coat, and resting behind on a sack filled with a gelatinous fluid. When the creature is alarmed it draws the eye back against the sack of fluid, which is thus forced into the folds of skin. They distend so largely as nearly to conceal the entire organ behind them. When swimming quietly along and suffered to be undisturbed, it generally remains so near the surface that its elevated dorsal fin projects above the water. Only in warm, calm weather is it seen in this attitude. During a stormy season it remains near the bed of the sea, and contents itself with feeding on the sea-weeds which grow so luxuriantly at the bottom of the shallower ocean waters. The color of the sunfish is grayish brown, darker upon the back than on the sides of the abdomen. The skin is hard and rough. The fish often attains a very great size. One that was harpooned on the equator measured six feet in length.

October 3, 1893, the following party went in the "Fannie G.": W. S. Eaton, F. D. Rogers, George Thayer, Joseph F. Fowler, F. H. Little, Mr. Haines, Mr. Bright, Mr. Pike, Mr. A. G. Sawyer, and myself. We had good sport and got a fine lot of game. The same party were out on several fishing trips with me, and we always had good luck. The fresh lobsters on board were a big luxury and highly enjoyed by us all.

CHAPTER XX.

THE FIRST TOW-BOAT IN PORTLAND.—CHANGED CONDITIONS OF OCEAN TRAFFIC.—THE BLUE SHARK AND HIS PURSUIT.—WILD GEESE SHOOTING. A NOTABLE SWORD-FISH PARTY.—THE FIRST PRIZE IN NINE YEARS.—LAST DEEP-SEA FISHING TRIP FOR THE SEASON.

THE first tow-boat owned in Portland was the "Tiger," built in Philadelphia, for my brother William, in 1851. She commenced towing in this harbor in November of that year. The first month was a busy one for him. During that time he towed two ships out of the Kennebunk River, and one out of the Saco. As the Cuba trade was flourishing then, the towing business was quite brisk. He was often called to Yarmouth, Freeport, and Brunswick to tow ships from their launching ways to this city, where they would complete their outfits for sea and sail for a Southern port to load cotton for the European market. Before the "Tiger" arrived here the vessels in want of a tow-boat had to send to Bath or Boston, and the "Tiger" received a welcome greeting by the ship-builders about Casco Bay.

At that time there were some fifteen or twenty ship-yards between Capes Elizabeth and Small Point. When the "Tiger" was built there were very few propeller tow-boats. Side-wheel tow-boats did this work then at New York, Philadelphia, and Baltimore. They are things of the past now, though a few are used for North River towing in shallow water. Times have changed. Not one ship is building from Cape Cod to

TOW-BOAT "TIGER," THE FIRST TOW-BOAT IN PORTLAND, CAPT. WILLIAM WILLARD. BUILT IN PHILADELPHIA, 1851.

Eastport. Three four-mast schooners and a steamer are building in Bath for the coasting trade, but nothing for the foreign. As the manufacturing business increases so does the coasting trade. We have a large fleet of coasting vessels employed principally in the ice, coal, phosphate rock, and hard pine trade. Steamers do all the general merchandise freighting. The towing business has increased so that four tow-boats and three water boats find employment in our harbor.

Wooden ships have gone out of date. Steel and iron steamers of European nations are doing most of the foreign freighting business. They have been built by subsidies; their government paying liberally what is called mail aid. In 1893 the five great Maritime Powers of Europe, England, France, Germany, Russia, and Italy, paid $16,657,865 for the transportation of their mails by sea. This not only builds their mail ships, but at the same time the subsidized companies have large fleets of the so-called tramp steamers, or freight ships, running in connection with their mail ships. Several of these lines have eighty to ninety steamers owned by each company. During the winter season, when the St. Lawrence River is closed by ice, the Allan and Dominion lines of steamers do a large freighting business to England and Scotland, taking freight from the Grand Trunk Railroad brought from all parts of Canada and the Western States.

BLUE SHARK.—The blue shark, which I have before mentioned, are the most common here and are seen in very large numbers on our coast in the summer. They are of a fine slaty-blue color on the back, and white on the belly, and are from three to fifteen feet long. They are the fishermen's most deadly enemy, cutting their nets to pieces and devouring their fish. Eight or nine of these monsters have been taken in one day. In the foreground of the engraving on page 96 is introduced the skull of a large shark for the purpose of showing the terrible teeth with which it is armed, and which lie in several reserve rows ready to take the place of those which are broken or cast off when their work is done. From these teeth, which cut like broken glass, the natives of many savage lands make tools and weapons of war by fixing them into wooden handles.

A friend of mine was once fishing after a large shark which was following the vessel. After a little time he succeeded in inducing him to take hold of the great hook which was fastened on the end of a large chain and nicely baited with a big, fat piece of pork of which these fish are very fond. Too sudden a jerk was given the hook, however, and it pulled through the cheek, which made a terrible cut and bled profusely. But the shark did not seem to mind that, for he kept right close up to the bait, which after a short time he finally seized and was drawn on board.

SHOOTING WILD GEESE AT HIGH PRESSURE.— In the spring of 1894, about the last of March, wild geese were reported very plentiful in Casco Bay. I got Mr. John F. Randall and Mr. J. N. Martin and steamed down the bay in the "Fannie G." We saw plenty of them feeding on the mussel beds. The water being shoal we could not get near them. We found that some had alighted in the bay, and so got to the windward and steamed towards them. They flew out of the water a long distance ahead and we got one of them. A day or two later Mr. Randall, his son, and myself went down the bay and got three more. We found that our steam from high pressure frightened

PEAKS ISLAND 1884.

them before we could get in shooting distance. Since that time I have put low pressure in the boat so to steam on to them without any noise.

THE FIRST SWORD-FISH IN NINE YEARS. — August 1, 1894, I started for a deep-sea-fishing trip in the "Fannie G." with the following party: W. J. Spicer, general manager of the Grand Trunk Company; W. A. Spicer, Charles Spicer, Errol Spicer, Herbert Spicer, all from Detroit; Doctor Alloway, of Montreal; Mr. Day, consul at Washington, D. C.; Rev. James Hasty, of Cornwall, Ontario; Capt. B. F. Woodbury, William Taylor, J. F. Randall, Joseph F. Fowler, George Thayer, of the Maine Central, Capt. H. E. Willard, and F. H. Little.

The party was prepared to catch anything from a whale to a mackerel. If you have never caught a sword-fish you do not know what fun and excitement are connected with the sport. The boat left the Grand Trunk Wharf at eight o'clock in the morning and proceeded to Peaks Island to get Captain Woodbury and friends. From there they went to Cushing's Island to get Mr. Spicer and his company. From Cushing's the steamer went over to Cape Cottage for a supply of fresh lobsters previously arranged for. We then put to sea.

About an hour was spent in fishing for cod on Rock Cod Ledge. In that short time over sixty cod were caught, some of them weighing twelve pounds. But that was not what the party was after; and with visions of sword-fish still before their eyes, the fun of fishing for cod seemed extremely tame. Beyond the ledge for a distance of eighteen or twenty miles to sea the little steamer went. The day was all that could be asked for. The water was smooth and calm, and the most sensitive ladies could have taken the trip so far as any danger from seasickness was concerned. Three hours after starting a shark was sighted. He was about seven feet long, and there was some desire to try to land him; but that desire was short-lived, for in a few moments a sword-fish was seen showing a back fin and tip of tail. Then the excitement ran high. Everybody was alive to observe the movements of the fish and the preparations for his capture. The steamer had been fitted to steam noiselessly on to the fish with low pressure, and so the game was not frightened by a noisy approach of the vessel. Captain W. took a position in the pulpit that Captain Peterson had built on purpose and stood with harpoon in hand till an advantageous position was reached. Then swish through the air the harpoon went, striking the big fish and burying itself some fifteen inches in his flesh. Rapidly the line was paid out to the length of one hundred fathoms or more, and a half-barrel thrown overboard with the line attached. Mr. Randall invited Mr. Fowler to sail on the half-barrel and watch the performance of the prisoner; but that gentleman declined, and so Mr. Sword-fish was allowed to hustle all by himself. In forty-five minutes the fish was on board. When he came up to the boat he made a struggle to get away, but Captain W. sent a second harpoon into him and that settled his fate. Mr. Randall made good use of the gaff and Captain Peterson got a tail rope on to the fish and another line around him for a parbuckle to roll him on board. Mr. Spicer and others had a hand on the upper deck and shortly the big fish was rolled on board, much to the delight of everybody.

This was the first sword-fish that "Captain Ben" had caught for nine years; and so the first thing to do when the capture was made and the excitement over was to ask Mr. Fowler to get the sarsaparilla so that he could take a good drink. Mr. Fowler suggested a pop cocktail, which used to be a favorite drink of the captain's; and then something stronger was offered, but the captain declined.

Everybody partook of the hot coffee and steamed fresh lobsters, and the boat again got under way for another sword-fish. At 1.30, when heading for Boon Island, the outlook saw another sword-fish and Captain W. sent the harpoon after him. When the steamer came around it left the fish on the port side, and the chances of striking fair with the harpoon were much lessened. The steel struck the fish a few inches higher than was at first intended, striking against the backbone so that when the line became taut the harpoon drew out and the fish drifted away to die and be eaten by the dogfish. Three hours more were spent in looking for fish, but with no good result. The boat got back at 5.45 P.M., all hands well pleased with the day's sport. The fish caught was twelve feet long and weighed two hundred and fifty pounds. The sword was three feet long and the tail three feet wide. The one lost was about seventeen feet long with a large body. It might weigh about five hundred pounds.

LAST TRIP OF THE SEASON.—August 17, 1894, I took my last deep-sea-fishing trip for the season with the following gentlemen: Mr. W. S. Eaton, F. D. Rogers, F. H. Little, B. F. Woodbury, George Thayer, K. D. Awtood, H. E. Willard, and William M. Leighton. The day was fine. We left Portland at eight o'clock in the morning. When near Portland Head we came to a fisherman and got all the fresh lobsters that we wished. Then we steamed for Rock Cod Ledge, stopping there something over an hour. We got sixty nice cod-fish; Mr. Eaton catching the largest one, about thirteen pounds in weight. While there fishing a school of mackerel came up and we caught thirty. We then steamed eighteen or twenty miles to sea looking for sword-fish. We steamed some sixty-five miles in all, but saw none. They had probably left the coast. We arrived home about six o'clock in the evening, after having a fine sail and nice sport.

CHAPTER XXI.

TRANSIT BETWEEN THE CAPE AND PORTLAND. — THE FAMOUS FERRY FIGHT. — A STORMY TOWN-MEETING. — THE DINNER THAT COST FIVE HUNDRED DOLLARS A PLATE. — CAPE ELIZABETH ELECTRICS. — THE ISLAND TRAFFIC AND THE CASCO BAY STEAMBOAT COMPANY. — PORPOISES.

THE ferry between Portland and Cape Elizabeth has given rise to both litigation and legislation, and is still a much discussed topic.

At my first coming from the Cape to Portland Captain Stanford ran a sail boat. I remember well the foresail — braided up. The boat was a large yawl and a safe one, and the captain a prudent man. He built a walk way from high water to low water, and could often be seen carrying a bucket of sand to sprinkle upon it to make the footing of his passengers surer.

This yawl was succeeded by a double-end ferry-boat named the "Elizabeth." At the time there was considerable ship-building, a chain factory was running, and a box mill in operation; so that the number of passengers was considerable. I understand that the "Elizabeth" paid fair dividends until Portland Bridge became free. Then she ceased to be profitable and the enterprise died. The "Elizabeth" was succeeded, after a brief experience with sail boats, by another double-ender, the "Little Eastern," and she died, too, in a short time.

Then still another double-ender, the "H. H. Day," was put on the ferry with sail boats running between times. After running for a while and failing to pay she was taken off. The town of Cape Elizabeth, I believe, helped to support her. On one of her trips from the Cape side on which I was a passenger, when half-way over to the city — the wind being heavy west northwest — the steam began to run down because of leaking tubes, putting the fire nearly out in the fire-box, and she went to leeward fast, toward the breakers near the Breakwater. The captain saw a coaster lying at anchor, made for her, with the intention of getting a line fast, having a man ready with a rope with an eye-splice in it. When we bumped up against the coaster he jumped on board and put the rope on the windlass bit. At the same time the captain of the schooner came on deck bare-headed. To say that he was mad would be to put it mildly. He jumped down over the deck load to heave off the line, but there was too much strain on it. The captain of the double-ender partially pacified him by saying that he would keep the wheels going ahead. The coaster had both anchors ahead by this time. If the chains had parted both vessels would have gone ashore in the breakers, and I do not know what would have become of us, as there was no life-saving crew stationed on the Cape at that time. I had supposed the double-ender had anchors, but saw none, and no preparations were made to get any either.

After another siege with sail boats, steam was again brought into requisition. Randall & McAllister bought the steamer "Josephine Hoey" to run as a ferry-boat and I unfortunately became a quarter owner. While she was running there came a northeast snow-storm and washed away the landing at the Cape. About six o'clock in the evening the ladies and gentle-men came down to go across as usual. I told them there was no landing and we could not run the boat, but I would take them to their destination safely, though it would have to be an overland trip. The company furnished hacks and took them over free of charge. I remember the night well, as I sat on the box with the driver, holding a lantern that we might find the way. We made two trips. When the last man got out of the hack he thought he ought to have ten cents for a drink, the drive had made him so dry.

Some time later the steamer "Mary W. Libby" was built to run in the winter and used in the summer for pleasure parties.

THE FERRY FIGHT.—In the winter of 1885 what is known as "the ferry fight"—into the particulars of which I need not go—began, and many of us were called before the committee of interior waters to testify. During the hearing my friend Mr. D—— stated that the "Josephine Hoey" was a "thin skin" boat, and he did not think she was safe to carry passengers across Fore River. Had he known her history he might have thought otherwise. The boat was brought here from New York by my brother Charles and R. W. Ricker, engineer, one stormy January. In rounding Cape Cod, between Chatham and Noset, she ran into a northeast snow-storm, blowing up a strong gale. In this blinding storm the boat made her way round the highland of the Cape, by Peaked Hill Bar and Race Point, found her way into Provincetown Harbor by use of the sounding lead, and anchored there about six o'clock in the morning. Some fishermen came down to the wharf and asked where she was from and of, and my brother told them from New York. "Did you come round the Cape last night?" they queried with astonishment. On his affirmative reply they informed him that two wrecks went ashore back of the highland and one on Peaked Hill Bar that night. That shows what a "thin skin" boat can do.

At the March meeting at the town-house, Cape Elizabeth, I invited my friend, C. W. T. Goding, to ride over with me to look on. Being a tax payer in that town, I supposed I had a right to go there, not to vote but to look on. From the time we arrived until we left we both were grossly insulted. I began to think we were among the "Mafias" of New Orleans. I had been a voter in Ward Two, Portland, for several years and had seen some rough times election days; but the election at Cape Elizabeth that year was far ahead of anything I ever saw. In the hands of Mr. Nutter was a document from our company to be read to the meeting. It was not allowed to be read. Had it been read and accepted the town would have been in pocket to-day $25,000, or the war debt might have been reduced that much. I am sorry to learn that the war debt still stands on the town books.

Later on our company received notice from the selectmen of the town to vacate the old landing in thirty days. We secured a temporary landing on the east side of Merchants' Marine Railway Wharf. I called on my friends to lease or buy a landing; but none was to be had. Later on our company found that Mr. Ralph Butler, of Boston, owned the flats at the east of Railway Wharf and we leased them of him for a term of years. Our company called on the harbor commissioners to lay out and build a wharf into tide water. To run our wharf straight it was found necessary to take a few feet on Mr. William Spear's property. Mr. Curtis and myself called on Mr. Spear to purchase a few feet of the flats; but he was very high in his figures so the company decided to put a bend in the wharf, in order to go around his land and save litigation. Then the wharf was extended into the water, giving seventy-five feet dockage between our wharf and Merchants' Marine Wharf. The wharf and ferry-house were built and the mud dredged out. We had a good, safe landing. June 4th of that year the double-end ferry-boat "Cornelia H." arrived from Bath and soon went on the route. She was a large and safe boat, but too good for the route. If Uncle Sam had known her butting qualities he would have given a large price for her to send out to Hayti instead of his gunboats, as she could have butted it all down in two hours. This ferry-boat ran about eight years. Then it changed hands and the new company built and put on the route the "Elizabeth City," now running.

There was lots of fun in the ferry fight, but no dividends.

I am glad to state the noted ten-year ferry fight came to a close April 1, 1895, by the Portland and Cape Elizabeth Ferry Company selling its franchise and ferry property to the People's Ferry Company. During the fight the Portland and Cape Elizabeth and People's Ferry Companies have taken out of their pockets about $130,000. This has been a very large elephant — much larger than Jumbo. Probably in the future one company will run the business.

THE BROOMSTICK TRAIN. I understand there is a company formed and about to get a charter to run an electric railroad through Cape Elizabeth by going over Portland Bridge, through Knightville, South Portland, Willard, and then over the shore road to the

Cape Lights. I think this is a move in the right direction. In two or three years it will build up the place and improve all property more than all the double-end ferry-boats have ever done from the days of the "Elizabeth" to those of the "Elizabeth City." If this road had been built after the big fire in Portland, in 1866, the Cape to-day would have a mayor as well as Deering. I wish to see the Cape built up.

A FIVE-HUNDRED-DOLLAR DINNER.—One day Mr. C. A. Tilton called at my office on Commercial Street to get subscribers for stock in the plush mill at South Portland. Though he fought us hard in the ferry fight we had no hard feelings towards him, but talked and laughed over the matter. Mr. John Curtis took five shares and I five. I don't consider it was all lost, as I got more out of it than some of my friends, and that was a good supper at the mill, which only cost $500 a plate.

THE ISLAND STEAMERS.—I wish to say a few words about the island steamers, a subject which interests all Portlanders. January 9, 1878, I bought into the Peaks Island Steamboat Company fifty shares. At this time Mr. F. H. Morse was President and George Trefethen, Treasurer. There were two steamers on the line, the "Express" and the "Gazelle." After a time the company became the Forest City Steamboat Company. The steamer "Gazelle" was lengthened and rebuilt, and her name changed to the "Forest City." Some time later Capt. Howard Knowlton built the little steamer "Minnehaha," which afterwards was taken into the company and Captain Knowlton made general manager. Then the Union

Steamboat Company was started as an opposition line to the Forest City Company. Their first boat was the "Emita," and their second, the "Cadet." Some time later the Union line changed to the Star Line Steamboat Company. At this time I was general manager for the Forest City Company. The Star line, after running two or three years, consolidated with the Forest City Company. The name was changed to the Casco Bay Steamboat Company and Mr. C. W. T. Goding elected general manager.

July, 1887, the company put on a new steamer, called the "Forest Queen." She is a large, safe boat and is run the year round. The steamers "Minnehaha" and "Express" were sold. January, 1884, the large skating rink and the pavilion were built at Peaks Island. A large gasoline plant was put into the rink, and later it was lighted by electricity and furnished power and light for all the amusement buildings and wharves. The Casco Bay Steamboat Company has done as much or more than any company in advertising Casco Bay as a summer resort by running amusements and getting up novel attractions such as marine carnivals, marine explosions, balloon ascensions, and walking on the waves. These attractions bring thousands of people to the islands and make it interesting for the boarders at the different hotels; so much so that the demand is considerably in excess of the accommodation.

The company have done good service by running boats often and at low rates and have built up the island largely in the last few years.

In the summer of 1894 the steamer "Jeanette" was put on the route as an opposition boat and run for five cents fare by parties interested in the ferry fight.

CAPT. B. J. WILLARD TRAP SHOOTING, JUNE, 1895.

PORPOISES.—Upon the opposite page is a picture of a shoal of porpoises,—a fine sight often seen in mild weather along our coast from Florida to Newfoundland, and near the northern edge of the Gulf Stream, where the warm water at a temperature of from 72 to 78 suddenly changes in going one or two miles down to 67 or 57 degrees. Here in this cool water for miles the water appears to be alive with porpoises, as seen in the picture. The meat of the porpoise is not very palatable, though the liver fried in pork fat is a very dainty dish, especially after living on salt beef for some time. So the capture of a porpoise puts a broad grin on an old sailor's countenance, as he is then sure of a dainty morsel. A shoal of porpoises moves in a military order excepting when frightened. They swim from five to ten miles an hour; springing out of the water in a crescent shape, their tails seldom leaving the water. They are a fine sight from a vessel's mast-head as they skim along just under water. Old sailors call them puffing pigs. Their puffing is as loud as a man's voice and is very interesting to any one not used to hearing or seeing them, as large shoals of them make a continual puff, puff, as though run by machinery.

———

At this point, in my sixty-seventh year, I bring these recollections of a busy and somewhat adventurous life to a close, hoping that the reader may find as much entertainment in taking them up as I have found in setting them down; for it has been a pleasure to me to recall the happenings—some of them stirring, and none without interest—of the years covered by this volume; and I am persuaded that the pleasure will be

A SHOAL OF PORPOISES.

shared by many an old friend and neighbor and many an acquaintance. It may be, too, that strangers who live far from the sea will find in this plain story of life on the Atlantic coast, and of adventure on an element with which they are unfamiliar, something to strike their fancy or appeal to their sympathies.

So in conclusion I say "good-by,"—two words which mean, scholars tell us, "God be with you."

ADDENDUM.

THE family of Willard of Eastbourne, Sussex, England, surnamed Villard and originating from Caen, Normandy, has been seated in Sussex since the time of Edward III. A younger branch settled later in the southwesterly part of Kent, within a few miles of the borders of Sussex, and held an estate in the Hundred of Branchley and Horsmonden. There lived and died (in 1617) Richard Willard, father of Capt. Simon Willard, the colonist, who came over from Horsmonden to Boston in 1634 with wife and children. He settled at Cambridge, Mass., and is known to have been possessed of ample means. He was later one of the founders of Concord and was for thirty-five years a member of the General Court of the Colony. He made use of the arms given on the cover, which is copied from the American Heraldic Historical Rooms.

HORSMONDEN.—In the southwesterly part of Kent, within a few miles of the borders of Sussex, in the Hundred of Branchley and Horsmonden, in the lath of Aylesford, lies the quiet and retired parish of Horsmonden. It is forty miles southeast from London, in a rural, agricultural district, situate on no great thoroughfare and possessing no factitious or local advantages for progress in population and wealth. As villages of this class alter but little from century to century in our mother-land, a description of the present appearance of Horsmonden will probably give a pretty correct idea of its aspect at the beginning of the seven-

OAK TREE AT HORSMONDEN.

teenth century. A descendant of Simon Willard in the seventh generation visited the ancestral home in the summer of 1850. He may be the first of all the descendants after the second generation who has enjoyed this privilege. Indeed, we may be reasonably well assured of the fact when we state that the particular parish in Kent, the birth-place of Simon Willard, has long ago passed from the memory of his American descendants through some unaccountable negligence, and the genealogy was only retraced as lately as the year 1845 after industrious and persevering inquiry. From the interesting sketch of Horsmonden, which this gentleman has given, I make the following extracts, copied from the Willard Memoir by Joseph Willard, Esq.:

"The church is two miles distant from the village and quite on one side of the parish. It is a venerable and rather neat Gothic edifice of stone. Its age is not known, but the rector supposes from the style of architecture that it is about five hundred years old. It is with certainty the church in which young Simon Willard was baptized, and it was with much interest that I read in the parchment register of that church, in old English characters, the record of his baptism. Just at the entrance, in the floor of the principal aisle, is a tablet to the dead bearing the date of 1587; and over that stone Simon was, doubtless, borne to his baptism.

"Near the church is a most magnificent oak tree, of which the men of Horsmonden are justly proud. The trunk is thirty feet in circumference at the roots and retains a circumference of nearly twenty feet almost to the branches. I was told at the rectory that it is known to be at least three hundred years old, and how much older is not known. Our ancestor in his boyhood doubtless looked upon it often and probably sat under its shade. Simon Willard, the subject of this sketch, was born at Horsmonden, probably in the early part of the year of 1605, and was baptized in the church at that place April 5, 1605. The record of his baptismal consecration, as recorded in the parish register and on a preceding page, runs thus wise:

"A. D. 1605. ANNO E. R. JACOBI.

"The vijth day of April Simon Willard come of Richard Willard was christened.

" EDWARD ALCHINE, Rector.

" Major Simon Willard died in Charlestown, Mass., April 24, 1676, in the seventy-second year of his age. The father, Richard Willard, died in February, 1616. He had ten children, seven of whom survived him. His third wife died on the 25th of February of the same year."

HORSMONDEN CHURCH, WHERE SIMON WILLARD WAS CHRISTENED, APRIL 5, 1605.

www.ingramcontent.com/pod-product-compliance
Lightning Source LLC
Chambersburg PA
CBHW021732220426
43662CB00008B/808